My Work Here is Done!

More Highly Random Essays on Weighty Matters

Scott Robinson

For my dear friend Laura Walter,

of whose travels I am envious,

and for whose friendship I am ever grateful

Also by Scott Robinson ...

The Beatles Guide to Love & Sex

To the Toppermost of the Poppermost:

    Exploring the Chart-Topping Hits of the Beatles

Rock Candy: The Beatles

The Quotable Beatles

YesTales: An Unauthorized Biography of Rock's Most Cosmic Band

Red Brains, Blue Brains: Neuroscience and Donald Trump

Red Brains, Blue Brains: Authoritarian We Will Go!

Lucy's Courtship: The Role of the Feminine in Human Evolution

Chasing the Enterprise:

    Achieving *Star Trek*'s Vision of the Human Future

Really Great Things That I Didn't Say

Uncle Scott's Treasury of Useless Knowledge

Uncle Scott's Treasury of Random Information

This is What I'm Saying: Burdens of a

    Midwestern Suburban Polymath

Shadows of Shadows

Table of Contents

Introduction

In the early days of personal computing we had a word – *wizzy-wig* – that told us a device or a software package was as advertised… nothing more, nothing less. *Wizzy-wig* was how we pronounced the almost-acronym WYSIWYG, which stood for What You See Is What You Get.

Minds work this way, too. Pay close attention, and even the most duplicitous discourse provides evidence of some repository of distinct and fathomable ideas, sweet or salt. Each of us is such a repository, a cauldron of ideas, acquired accidentally or intentionally (inevitable some of each), and the contents of our personal repository is ultimately what defines us.

The human capacity to ponder, to take in thoughts from others and allow them to reshape our own, sets us apart. In pondering, we change, we grow, we confront one another on the landscape of the mind. Too often, this confrontation is exactly that, a flurry of defense and barriers. Too seldom, we open ourselves to new thoughts, inviting others in, setting aside what we no longer need to carry.

The pages that follow are offered in that spirit. With any luck, they will set pondering in motion, and whatever is of value on the page will be improved, when added to the thoughts of you, the reader.

"In diversity, you can trace certain properties of
the human spirit that transcend differences. It is
only when you look at what unites humans rather
than what divides them that you have some idea
of what it means to be human."

~ Gene Roddenberry

Knowledge

Knowledge is empowerment.

Knowledge is accomplishment.

Knowledge is comfort.

It is protection. It is exploration. It is discovery, expansion.

It is an asymptote - forever approaches, never fully achieved.

It quietly strengthens, and gradually protects.

It need not be acquired in the pursuit of industry, or utility, or even security; it loses none of its value when pursued for no sake but its own.

It leads away from confusion and toward wisdom.

It deepens awareness of others, and especially of self.

It is the embrace of reality.

It is acquired with ease, but inculcated only with great effort.

It is among our earliest hungers, and our final abdications.

The Many Human Natures

One of the biggest stumbling blocks in human social organization is the institutional myth that there is only one "human nature" - that all human beings think and act within the same cognitive and behavioral range. This is demonstrably untrue, and the myth has caused staggering damage to human societies over the millennia - but still it persists.

One institutional position on human nature can be found in the holy texts of the patriarchal religions, which holds that human beings are innately "evil" beings, born into the world with a predisposition for greed, deceitfulness, and a propensity for violence.

Another is entrenched in our contemporary economic theory - that human beings are innately selfish as individuals, rather than egalitarian and reciprocal.

Still another is that human beings are naturally good, born loving and selfless, and are beaten down in childhood into the untrusting and unhappy citizens that populate our offices and neighborhoods.

None of these are correct, per our understanding of human brains and the minds they enable. There is not a single "human nature"; there are many, and each gives rise to a person with a distinct point of view of self and others, who will act in the world and within groups in distinct ways that will differ from those of different nature.

Is this truly distinct human nature, or just personality variation? That's a valid question, one we'd be careless to skip over. To get at the answer, we have to do two things: assess the full range of thought and action that these distinctions encompass, and see if the variations are sufficient to break our single-nature models.

At one end of the thought/action range, human beings appear to be socially level, embracing equality within the tribe; risk-takers, unafraid of the unknown; explorers who need to see what's over the hill. At the other end, human beings appear to be vertically organized, following a single alpha; they are cautious, untrusting of the world; and they are territorial, more interested in borders than horizons.

This sounds like two completely different species, doesn't it? And these are just two extreme points in a multidimensional space: there are many mix-and-match variations of human nature in between.

Do these truths break our models of human nature? Let's start with the patriarchal religious models.

It takes but an hour of online RSS feed surfing to turn up multiple Christianities: some view Christ as the great equalizer, "bringing down the Mighty" and "lifting up those who are of low degree" - essentially a progressive liberal, concerned with the plight of the poor. Others view Christ as their violent champion, embracing his statement, "Do not suppose that I have come to bring peace to the earth. I did not come to bring peace, but a sword" - militant and partisan to the core, poised to lay waste to enemies.

These two Christs (and there are, of course, many in between) are as opposite as can be, and each attracts persons of completely different natures. And so it is with every patriarchal faith.

And finally, there is the model of human nature built into our economic systems, inspired by the agnostic philosophers of the 17th and 18th centuries, which holds that humans are rational beings who act from cold calculation: that each one is pondering and acting to his personal advantage, within the pool of human labors and pursuits.

National economies have been driven by these assumptions for more than two centuries, and they've been taken for granted by the powerful and influential throughout that term. But we now systematically and dispassionately observe these behaviors close-up, and - it just isn't true. *Human beings act against their own self-interest almost perpetually.* This stands out starkly in democratic elections, but can be observed in almost every sector of economic life: most people mismanage their own self-interest, from mating choices to occupational training to spending to voting.

Is this due to a lack of education and understanding of economics? the staggering complexity of our systems, perhaps? Whatever those factors contribute to the dysfunction, they aren't decisive; all the necessary information to live one's life with true self-interest and strategic advantage is readily available (and some people do choose to make use of it), but most people simply don't care enough to invest the effort. This has been studied in-depth for decades, and the verdict is simple: some human beings do indeed live strategically, but far more are scattered around the spectrum, pursuing those acts and choices that bolster their sense of self, or satiate their emotions in the moment.

There is a big Why to all of this, and it's rooted in our evolution, and we've talked about it elsewhere: human beings thrived while competitors

withered *precisely* because we vary so much in the area of "human nature";
other, more linear species were less socially bonded and, in the long run,
less adaptable, and so they are no more.

The idea that there is just one "human nature," then, is toxic; it delivers
inadequate social systems, inequality-driven economies, and poor levels of
social cooperation. *The reason we've lasted this long is our diversity.* Any
thoughts that diminish it are to our ultimate detriment, not our ultimate
advantage.

Freedom and Uncertainty

The formal study of Authoritarianism by social scientists began after World War II, which was of course one of history's greatest exemplars of its dangers. But even before this study began, psychologist Erich Fromm weighed in.

In 1941, he published *Escape from Freedom*, a book that explored the notion that many populations under Authoritarian rule *want* to be; many people are more comfortable surrendering their lives and well-being to an autocrat than living in freedom.

How can this be?

It is, in fact, simple: evolving in a complex and uncertain world, human brains express a range of social response to that uncertainty. Many existential dangers threaten the individual human, and many more threaten the endurance of human groups. There are, of course, no guarantees at either level - life is precarious, and always has been, and always will be. Uncertainty is built into human existence.
That range of response runs from openness to that uncertainty to a deep dread of it. There are many among us who are untroubled by the idea of a precarious future, and others who find it utterly terrifying (most of us live somewhere in between). That's perfectly natural; that's how we're built. That range empowers us, collectively.

But freedom - the decision to operate laterally, giving individuals the liberty to decide for themselves - breeds uncertainty. It multiplies, at both the individual and group levels, the possible outcomes in the human march - and the uncertainties, as well. To be freedom-loving is to embrace uncertainty, or at least be at peace with it.

Freedom has the opposite effect on the uncertainty-adverse. Freedom amplifies the terrifying noise of the world, in the ears of Fromm's supplicant masses; they want it to stop. They want someone to stand between them and the dark mists of incertitude. They will surrender whatever they must, to have that person between them and danger.

Such people are perfectly understandable, when viewed through this lens. Moreover, they are impossible to despise, let alone fear; they come by their feelings very naturally. To mock and demean them is not only inappropriate but counterproductive; far better to understand, and try to sympathize...

...and, all the same, keep a close eye on whomever they are standing behind.

Opposition

We can oppose the Authoritarian rhetoric and threatening behaviors of a socially dominant leader and his followers without descending into threatening rhetoric and behavior ourselves, and without dialing up daily heapings of scorn and derision. In fact, it is essential - maybe even survival-critical - that we stop.

There's an emotional appeal to be made here, but let's start with reason:

1. Responding to threatening rhetoric and behavior with oppositional rhetoric and behavior makes us feel good, but we can easily see and know objectively that it has no substantive effect; faced with opposition, the authoritarian feels not shame but pride. The anger and disapproval only fan the flames of self-righteousness. This doesn't diminish the problem, it intensifies it. We all understand this from past experience, but we dial up our emotions and our oppositional bellowing anyway - because it makes US feel self-righteous.

2. The catch is that the authoritarian leader and follower behave as they do for reasons both neurophysiological and sociological; they truly *believe*they are righteous, that those who oppose them are foolish and wrong and even evil. To feel the same is to be mired in the same ignorance of human nature that they are. To interpret the authoritarians' emotions for them and to assign them a moral score, as they do us, is a complete waste of energy; it only distracts from authentic, effective understanding. Shouting down their feelings and motivations and reasoning is like shouting on the weather, and about as useful.

3. When we respond to the authoritarian leader and followers in their own voice, hollering about their hypocrisy and immorality and evil, we weaken ourselves. By choosing this path, rather than calm and systematic political and social action to counterbalance their efforts, we allow ourselves to slip into feeling threatened by their behaviors - and when we feel threatened, our attention narrows (irrationally) and our available brainpower and social motivation constrict. Put another way, by responding emotionally to the authoritarians, we deprive ourselves of the personal resources to meaningfully do something about them.

None of this is meant to diminish anyone's right to feel as they do - that would be foolish, by the very definitions set forth above. Instead, the point is to put both the stimulus and response in perspective, and hopefully encourage the setting of an alarm in every non-authoritarian head - an alarm that says, *Whups, I'm getting riled, and that won't help*; I need to see these people more clearly, respond less angrily, and focus my attention on actions that will truly make things better...

Death in the Family

I recently stood in the Atlantic surf as someone close to me spread the ashes of someone close to her on the waters. I was reminded, with a quiet trembling, of how close my oldest son came to death when an SUV struck him at 45 mph as he was on foot. We were told to expect the worst, or that he would lose his right leg at the very least. Four surgeries and three months later, my son walked out of the hospital, though he will never play basketball or tennis again. I'll never forget the pain of that night, or the following weeks.

But the one standing with me in the surf suffered far more. To love someone intimately, especially one's own child, and lose them unexpectedly and forever - I can imagine nothing worse. Yet most of us suffer such a loss, at one point or another in our lives.

It occurs to me that this is yet another province of the social brain where today is unlike yesterday. Our life expectancy in the prehistoric past, as best we are able to measure it from here, would have been somewhere between 19 and 25. So most if not all human beings suffered loss of close family far more frequently than we do.

Why is this so? The Cro-Magnon human is biologically programmed for the same lifespan we are. Why die so early?

Because of disease? No, pandemics arrived when we began clustering in one place, in the hundreds and then thousands, bringing on disease through perpetual close proximity with animals, using stale water and taking up weak dietary practices.

Because of each other? No, we were more peaceful in the ancient past than we are today - more dependent upon one another, with a greater stake in one another's success. We invented war when we invented property.

Because of starvation? No, we ate 300-400 different things before we invented agriculture; if one food was in short supply, there was plenty of something else at hand. We were far healthier then than we are today. We lived brief lives because we ourselves were food.

For 99% of the term of our genus, and 90% of our term as a species, we were food for large predators, the apex lords of the savannah - cats twice the size of modern lions, who picked us off easily whenever we strayed beyond our tribe. We have found many caches of human bones in the long-abandoned caves of such cats in south-central Africa; we have found human skulls punctured by large feline teeth.

Our leading cause of death, and the reason so few of us went elderly, was predation - our survival was measured by our ability to avoid it - easier to do in large groups, with emerging technologies like spears and fire, but ultimately a measure of our alertness and personal speed.

Imagine, for a moment, living in that routine pattern of loss - a parent vanishing, a sibling taken down while gathering, and most horrifically, a small child carried off.

These are terrifying thoughts, especially ugly in the context of contemporary grief. But I mention it to make a point: grief is a function of the ancient human brain, highly developed in ourselves and in the other higher mammals. Why? Grieving, and the sharing of it, serves to bond the group more deeply when loss occurs. We retain the trait, of course, but it's worth noting that while we suffer loss far less often than our Paleo ancestors did, we also run the risk of letting our grief pass too quickly, as it often goes unshared - and we lose a few threads of connection that nature would have us weave between us.

As I stood there in the surf, next to a parent whose lost child is now five years past, I realized I was seeing exactly this: a daily remembrance, a seasonal reflection - a weaving of grief that serves to bond and strengthen - and which honored me with participation, however peripheral. I'll never see grief, or the comfort it requires, the same way again.

Country Folk and City Slickers

I recently read a wonderful book, *The Big Sort: Why the Clustering of Like-Minded America is Tearing Us Apart*, by Bill Bishop. As you might guess, that book explores themes that are close to my heart.

It brings into high relief the cognitive distinctions between people who tend to settle into the countryside, vs. those who prefer city life. Rural citizens, as a general rule, cluster into smaller communities with greater familiarity, some resistance to change, and a strong sense of community loyalty. City people, on the other hand, have looser social ties, are more opportunistic, and are often attracted to novelty and change.

Aren't the rural people practicing Paleolithic community, with their smaller communities and deeper relationships?

Aren't the city people anti-Paleo, with their more casual bonds and greater numbers (less Dunbar brain space)?

Isn't this an interesting problem? Here's how it breaks down:

Yes, the rural communities are more Dunbar-like in their numbers; and yes, they are more Paleo in their social bonds.

But if we're going thru this door, we have to think it through all the way, and this gives us a demonstration of how the axes of social cognition interact with one another. Rural people are more focused on strong social ties - but those ties are clustered ties; they resist risk and novelty, and so make less robust community choices and decisions. City people are less socially bonded, but are more cognitively diverse; they are better able to explore new ideas and make more robust decisions.

This toss-up of Paleo community traits gets even more complex in Bishop's reading of the evolution of big cities in the US. The film industry, for instance, *should* have emerged in New York City, where the resources for it were already concentrated; instead, it happened in a small LA suburb.

Why?

Per Bishop, it's because NYC hosts a society and an economy based on strong and complex social structures - a hierarchy that must be accommodated for anything to get accomplished. No such structures existed in early 20th century Hollywood.

Similarly, how did Silicon Valley come to be? It was a vast plain of fruit orchards in the early Fifties. Why didn't high tech also emerge in the Northeast, where the big money of corporate America resided at the time?

Why Silicon Valley? Because the community dynamic of Big Business is antithetical to innovation: novelty cannot be easily accommodated in rigid social hierarchies, where mobility is sharply constrained and change happens slowly by design. Novelty thrives when social boundaries are weak and opportunity is abundant.

And here are two huge factors, both with strong Paleo support: city life is inherently more migratory, and Opportunity Scanners and Novelty Seekers embrace that impulse; and places like Hollywood and Silicon Valley present tremendous Common Purpose, doorways into collective social achievement that bind groups for years, working and living together constantly until the purpose is achieved (the making of *Gone With the Wind* and the evolution of the Mac both consumed roughly the same number of years as a Paleolithic adulthood). And once a particular territory of Common Purpose has been explored - the tribe moves on, mixing and matching members in a fruitful cross-training of minds.

The point is this: the social features of City Thinking and Rural Thinking all trace back to our ancient origins, and those features display both strength and weakness in the modern era. The lesson to us is to fully understand and appreciate them, and push back against their tendency to divide us.

Bambi is Just Wrong

Like so many of us, I grew up on Disney movies. And like so many of us, I was terrified, around age six, of the story of the young fawn in the big forest, growing to adulthood in the frightful shadow of Man.

It's a story of loss, as he grieves for his mother; a story of mortality, as he and his fellow creatures flee a raging forest fire. It's a coming-of-age tale to prepare six-year-olds everywhere for the horrors of adolescence and social ascendance.

It's the story of the emerging Great Prince of the Forest.

"Bambi."

Does that sound right? Really?

"Bambi" is what you expect to hear when you're introduced to a well-endowed stripper. "Bambi" is a name that evokes sequins and tassels. "Bambi" is as feminine a name as one is likely to hear in the actual world – and not simply feminine, but erotic.

Per Disney, however, Bambi is not a female, but a male; and not just a male, but an *alpha* male; and not just an alpha male, but the *Great Prince of the Forest*.

Work with me here. Let's try it out here in the actual world. The stripper's name isn't Bambi, it's Faline (Bambi's future mate in the movie); some guy is giving her a hard time, so she needs the bouncer to remove him. She says to another stripper, "I need some help here! Get Bambi, quick!"

Taking it up a notch or two, let's track down the alpha male in that part of town - the leader of the roughest, toughest gang: "Yeah, that's me, I be Bambi. Who wantstaknow?"*And these other two gentlemen?* "He be my man Thumper. And him, he be Flower."

Let's try it out at the national level: "Good evening and welcome to Smackdown, here at the Wells Fargo Center in Philadelphia, where The Beast, Brock Lesnar - the man who took down The Rock! - will face the most dangerous opponent of his career: Bambi!"

See, for me, names matter. Names convey an impression, and often an emotion. Presidents can be named James and John and Frank and Tom and Ted and Abe and Ben and even Ulysses. Those are all strong, masculine names, right? Barack, sure, with that strong "k" sound at the end. And you can get away with Bill and Richard and Harry and Andy, they sound warm and friendly and neighborly. George? Hm, okay, I guess. But can we agree that Lyndon is kind of sissy-fied? Dwight? Warren? Calvin? Ronald? "Millard?" - please. And Grover, well, that's a Muppet name.

But wouldn't we take *any* of those over Bambi? Could a Bambi, no matter his qualifications, experience or degree of personal masculinity, ever be Leader of the Free World?

Names matter. They convey an impression in advance of actual introduction, they set the stage. And giving the Great Prince of the Forest a moniker better suited to a state university sorority girl leaves the young viewer of this classic film waylaid, lulled into a false sense of innocuous cuteness that renders the horrors to come all the more brutal.

It's 75 years now since Bambi debuted in theaters. It's due for a remake. Let's fix this problem now, and invoke the gratitude of countless future generations. Let's tell Disney we want the Great Prince of the Forest, and call him Macho Man. Or The Big Red Monster. Or Barack.

"Hello, babies! Welcome to Earth. It's hot in the summer and cold in the winter. It's round and wet and crowded. On the outside, babies, you've got a hundred years here. There's only one rule that I know of, babies - Goddamn it, you've got to be kind."

~Kurt Vonnegut, *God Bless You, Mr. Rosewater*

We Just Dance

My friend Laura, to whom this book is dedicated, heard a talk by Joseph Campbell that included the story of a Western man who made his way to Japan. When he arrived, a native took him for a visit to a Shinto shrine. He perused, wandering about the shrine, soaking in its content, its architecture, its artifacts.

Pondering what he'd seeing, and struggling to comprehend it, he said to his host, "It's very lovely, but I don't get it. I don't get the ideology."

The native said, "There is no ideology. There is no theology. We just dance."

The Carpet and the Drapes

I feel it a matter of principle, as I am so free and loose with what I consider my best thoughts, that I openly confess my even-more frequent confusions and bafflements. The list of these is lengthy, and many of the puzzles that have confounded me over the years have remained, like liver spots in my brain, unyielding in the face of endless contemplation.

One such puzzle presented itself when I was a younger man and had met a perky, fun young woman with a sharp mind, intense gaze and a lively blonde mane. I met her one evening at a local club, when she was with a couple of her friends and I had dropped in to hear the band that was playing that weekend.

We hit it off and began dating. But I could tell this could go somewhere, so I stepped up my attendance at the club, hoping to run into her - any excuse to see her!

There sat her two friends, chatting. They didn't see me, so I slipped into the next booth, hoping for some covert intel.

They were talking about me!

"She says he really seems into her," one of them was saying. "How's he going to feel when he finds out that what he likes best about her came out of a bottle?"

"-when she gets him home," the other one said, "and he finds out the carpet doesn't match the drapes!" And they both laughed and laughed.

I'd hear this carpet-and-drapes thing before, and figured it was just another of those odd female obsessions, like shoes and toenails, that only makes sense to other women. I was mildly concerned about the "bottle" remark - was she a tippler? Was her jolly demeanor alcoholically inspired? I had seen no signs of this.

A couple of my friends were over the next afternoon, a Sunday, for football. I asked about this.

"Pete," I inquired, "does your wife care about the drapes?"

"Oh, hell, yes," he groaned. "It took her six weeks to make up her mind. She even sent one batch back after I'd wasted a weekend hanging them all. Cost me a damn fortune!"

I turned to the other. He nodded.

"Was it a color thing?"

"Color, texture," he said. "They had to be perfect. Had to match the sofa and love seat.And, of course, the carpet."

A-HA!!!

I turned back to Pete. He nodded.

"Ted," I said, "Did she care if *you* cared if the colors matched?"

He stared blankly. "I was never consulted."

"Ted," I asked carefully, "do you even know what color your carpet is?"

He thought a bit, and thought some more, and frowned. "I really have no idea," he finally confessed.

The next day, on the way home from work, I drove by her place - I hadn't yet been invited in - and surveyed the drapes hanging in the living room window. They looked like fine drapes to me. I had no idea what color they were. But they looked quite fine.

The following weekend I took her to a movie, and when I drove her home, she invited me inside for a drink.

"I've been so looking forward to having you here!" she confided as she dug out her house key.

"Me, too!" I said enthusiastically. "I've been dying to see if the carpet matches the drapes!"

She froze, and kind of stared at me, with an expression that was a clear mixture of fascination and horror. How can women do that? Go figure! I quickly deduced that she was not expecting this level of stylistic acuity in a man she'd only just met, so I just gave her a reassuring grin to set her at ease. She proceeded to unlock the door, albeit hesitantly.

Her place was much neater than mine, of course, and cheerfully decorated, with those extra pillows on the couch and inscrutable little sculptures on every shelf. I nodded approvingly as she stepped over to the bar to fix some drinks.

"The drapes I noticed right away," I commented, carefully stepping around the fact that I'd driven past her place earlier in the week (I didn't want to come across as creepy). "But I've had to settle for imagining the carpet!"

Once again she sort of froze, and I began to realize this was a sore spot - but I couldn't fathom why! I looked down at the carpet. It was a fine carpet, a truly homey, warm carpet. I was no more clear on the color of the carpet than the drapes, but if they clashed, I wouldn't have had a clue.

Handing me my drink, she gave me a nervous smile. "I'm not sure I've learned to tell when you're joking, or not," she said.

She put on an Oldies station and we sat on the couch chatting, having our drinks.

It needs to be said to women everywhere, of course, that men are completely oblivious to matters like this - like the shoes-and-toenails thing. We just have no clue, and wouldn't care, even if we did. When a man is invited in, the carpet and the drapes go right off his radar: he's just feeling lucky that he's in.

But this was not the moment. Clearly this *was* very important to her, of the utmost sensitivity; I had tripped an insecurity, and she needed reassurance.

"I want you to know," I smoothly segued during a lull, "that I have no doubts at all about your aesthetic sensibilities. I have trusted all along that your carpet and drapes would match. I can tell you're not the sort of woman who would bungle something that important."

She showed me the door, and firmly instructed me to lose her number. Go figure!

You can see, I hope, that your Uncle Scott is only human, and sometimes just doesn't get it. I did, however, learn much from the experience: the next time I meet a male interior decorator, I won't be so quick to mock...

History Can't *Not* Repeat

It's a cultural cliché that humankind can't seem to learn from history, that we see the same cycles endlessly repeating. Who would have thought, after the horrors of the Holocaust - our grandparents' time! - or the race riots of the Sixties - our parents' time! - that our own generation, after putting a dark-skinned man in the White House, would see the resurgence of white nationalism, the KKK, and flags with swastikas?

We should tuck our surprise away in a trunk somewhere. It was naive to believe that the election of Barack Obama or Mae Jemison making astronaut or the presence of Samuel L. Jackson in every movie made in the past 20 years meant the end of racial bigotry. The unfortunate truth is we misconceive the nature of racial bigotry to begin with; and failing to understand what it really is and what causes it, we have little chance of doing anything about it.

Let's summarize those failings.

Education hasn't fixed it. Decades of integrated schools, curricula that include strong themes on racial equality, our universal genetic heritage, and the inclusion of the accomplishments of minorities in our national history have done nothing to discourage the proliferation of hate groups.

The elevation of minorities into positions of prominence and power hasn't fixed it. Minority members appear now at all levels of government and business, albeit in weak ratios; if anything, this has only intensified the feelings of those who hate them.

Legislation hasn't fixed it. Efforts to level the playing field, defend the minority vote, and curb discriminatory behaviors in the justice system have not diminished the growing tide of white supremacy.

All of these fixed are important, but none of them address the core problem: discomfort with those who are different isn't an absolute in either direction; like so many human characteristics, it's highly variable. Some people are more naturally fearful of other people than others - it's the roll of the genetic dice. And when such people huddle together for years, their fear is greatly amplified, becoming anger.

These are two very difficult problems. We can never be rid of the first one - our genes will always deliver a certain number of people in any population who are more uneasy than others. The second one, moving to a societal model that diffuses like-mindedness, isn't impossible - there's just no clear answer, no obvious way to entice people to seek out differences in viewpoint for its own sake.

But I, for one, am not done trying.

Kindness is Viral

I sat and talked with my teenage daughter last night. She is my youngest, the baby of the family, and the apple of my eye. As is often the case with lastborns - I, the parent, have already made most of my mistakes, and am close to getting this parenting thing down - our Daddy/Daughter relationship is warm and trouble-free.

Not so in other relationships. Josie gets along far better with me than she does with her brother and mother. That's to her credit, not mine, but we both acknowledged it, and I thought about it afterwards.

Her mother and brother say that she is at her best around on me (and not them) because I dote on her and think she's still 6 and can't accept that she's almost fully grown.

All of that is perfectly true, of course, but I say it's because kindness is our default. My daughter is always sweet to me. I, in turn, want to treat her with all the kindness in the world.

Kindness begets kindness. When the guy behind the counter at the convenience store says, "Have a great day!", my reflex is to smile and say, "You, too!" When a mother with three kids holds the elevator door for me, I'm inclined to do the same when she and her brood set off. My server at the restaurant offers my kids a couple of desserts that will go to waste if someone doesn't take them - on the house. I tell him I don't need any change when I pay the bill.

The convenience store guy may have a confederate flag on his bumper. The mom-with-kids might believe that gay marriage is an abomination. My server might have voted for Trump. Would I have been so reciprocal with the three of them, had I known these things?

But *I didn't* know those things; the convenience store guy does not look me in the eye and declare, "The South will rise again!" The mom doesn't lean my way and say, "They're putting my marriage at risk!" The server doesn't lean down and whisper, "He's making America great again!" in my ear.

That's just not how the world works. The reality is that most of the people whom we encounter that we don't know and never will are simply Other Human Beings - neither red nor blue, neither straight nor gay, neither faithful nor apostate. Just Other Human Beings.

Josie and I know each other as well as family can; these strangers and I are at the opposite end of the intimacy spectrum. Yet here, too, kindness is the default.

And somewhere in the middle, there's the Internet - where we don't begin our encounters with strangers by saying, "Have a great day!", or offering an unsolicited kindness, or taking an interest for its own sake; no, we *lead* with "The South will rise again!" and "Republicans are cruel!" and "Atheists are destroying America!" and "Christian Taliban!"

On the Internet, we jump straight to the middle. The thing is...

There should *be* no middle.

That kindness that we enjoy as our default when we encounter a stranger, that we enjoy many years into a treasured relationship, should persist from Day One, ad infinitum. Can anyone give me a reason why not?

We should be as kind to those we love, many years on, as we are to the guy in the convenience store. Familiarity breeds contempt, the cliché goes, and that's certainly a struggle - but the Internet is making it our default.

I think it's time to move in the other direction. I think Josie and I are getting it right...

What Kind of Person Is This?

Having looked at the question of human nature, and how there really isn't one, all-inclusive "human nature," we begin to realize that we are surrounded by not just one "kind" of human being, but many.

Any of us, in our daily sojourn, encounters a vast array of different "kinds" of human beings. And these differences in kind have nothing to do with the color, gender, or social status of those other human beings.

Some people, as we've discussed, see all people as pretty much the same: "human being" is a category unto itself, and the variations within don't matter much; others see people as very different, some worthy of much and others worthy of little.

Some people crave change and progress, pursuing the new and different; others prefer the comforts of sameness, more at home at home. Some eschew risk, while others ignore it; some delight in surprise, while others embrace the familiar.

This gives us many different kinds of human being, and the differences, even among our immediate neighbors, go deeper than language and culture: they are differences that define how we enter the world and survive in it.

Failure to understand this, and failure to strive to relate to others across that boundary, is to fail in truly human connection, or to achieve real human community. But how do we get there? There's no easy way.

Reaching across the divide of "many minds," the consequence of our staggering cognitive variety, can't be achieved individually or in isolation. Even a strong intellectual grasp of the concept is not sufficient to enable a true personal understanding of the view from that other mountain. And a mountain it is: the accumulation of a person's lifetime of experiences, gathered through eyes trained by a mind of a certain kind, takes one to a place that is far removed from many if not most others, whose experiences and eyes are vastly different.

There is one way, and one way only: to merge one's experience with that of others, in pursuit of a view closer to theirs. Put another way, if I am to fully understand and appreciate and connect with this person who sees the world from another mountaintop, I must climb that mountain, too – or, at the very least, travel to its vicinity.

Psychologist Robert Altemeyer has studied this in depth, and in particular among young people of Authoritarian predisposition and training. His research shows that when students who have been raised as Authoritarian thinkers in Authoritarian communities (usually religious) are exposed to a wide variety of peers who think differently, their level of Authoritarian thought (measured when they first enter school) will decrease significantly over their time in school. To say it differently, we begin to see through the eyes of others when we put ourselves out there and experience the world alongside them.

And when we do more fully understand the differences between ourselves and the persons not like us whom we encounter, we will find ourselves handling each such encounter a little differently - adjusting our intent, our assessment, our expectations and our empathy accordingly, to the benefit of both.

This requires resolve. Commitment. A serious desire to bridge the divides between us. In prehistoric times, it wasn't a question; we lived and died among persons of all natures, and knew each intimately. We could not *not* bridge those divides. In modern times, it's all too easy; and if we fail to make those journeys, we diminish our own potential, and deny ourselves the full richness of the human experience.

"There's a reason you separate military and the police. One fights the enemies of the state, the other serves and protects the people. When the military becomes both, then the enemies of the state tend to become the people."

~Edward James Olmos, *Battlestar: Galactica*

Creating Steve Jobs

Part of my job is to comment on the technology industry. I have been interviewed many times for podcasts and am a columnist for an information technology magazine. And an interesting question has come up that touches on things we've covered in this book.

The question is this: As AI is now out-performing human beings at all kinds of tasks, and intelligent automation is taking over business processes in all domains, will it take over completely? Specifically, is there anything uniquely human about people-thought that machines cannot replace?

This ties not only into how brains work, but also into economies and human value. So I thought you'd all maybe take an interest.

My scientist friends and I are all disciples of the cognitive scientist Douglas Hofstadter, one of the most important voices in this field, who emphatically *does* believe that machines can ultimately replicate every nuance of human cognitive performance. Despite my love of Doug's work, I disagree. Here's why:

The computer was invented 75 years ago for a very distinct purpose: to do things well that human brains do very poorly. Specifically, we needed to do gargantuan mathematical operations very quickly, very repetitive work, at speeds beyond what our brains can achieve. The development of the computer has walked that road ever since: doing well what we do badly. And the converse has been true: the computer does badly what our brains do well (create art, make conversation, etc).

The line is blurring now because we have become competent in new ways of using math to understand behavior. We are able to do deep operations with contextual data surrounding events and behaviors that tell us more about the events and behaviors than we originally realized there was to know. And we use computers to do that new math (we call it *analytics*). So the computer has become our ally in understanding ourselves. That's a new thing.

Because of analytics, AI now seems more perceptive than we ourselves are; AI systems are able not only to handle very complex business operations and manage highly variable environments, they are also able to study their own performance (descriptive analytics), anticipate problems ahead of time (predictive analytics), and come up with improvements (prescriptive analytics).

The problem we get into is the illusion that this is all there is to intelligence. But the word 'intelligence' is like the word 'music' - it's a single word describing many things. The phenomenon of intelligence has many layers, and our AI systems address only a few of those layers.

Let's begin with a key human distinction: we are vessels of intelligent thought and agents of intelligent behavior. And those are not the same thing.

Business wants AI systems to execute intelligent behavior - to perform workflows, to implement tasks, to have agency. We could say that humans can innovate in performing tasks and machines can't, but that's rapidly becoming untrue: the business workforce is already threatened far more than anyone realizes by the rise of intelligent automation in the cloud. I comment on this on a monthly basis. Trust me, the desk worker is going the way of the factory worker, within a generation.

But intelligent thought is something else altogether, and machines can't even get onto that playing field. Arguing from the very top, let's imagine an AI as CEO of a technology company: imagine the company makes computers and has a reputation for innovation. But the innovation is gone, and the company is failing.

Installing an AI at the top would result in efficiency moves: slashing the workforce, reducing the product lines, getting the books back in balance. All well and good - only a handful of human CEOs could make a success of that.

But could the AI then diversity the company into creating an entirely new market - consumer tech? Could it have the idea to branch its computer technology into digital music platforms with portable devices, create keyboard-free, hand-held Internet utilities? Would it have the idea to turn cellphones into digital app platforms?

In short, an AI can't be Steve Jobs. And it can't be Steve Jobs because we can't recreate what made Steve Jobs Steve Jobs in workflows, or uncover those uniquely human features with analytics? Why not? *Because we can't observe those things.*

We can't build Steve Jobs - or HAL-9000, for that matter - because that means replicating human thought as well as human behavior. And we are learning, to our chagrin, that the neurological foundation of human thought is far, far deeper and more complex than our conscious ruminations. A quick tour of Sam Harris's recent writings will illuminate the fact that most of the thoughts that actually rise to the level of conscious deliberation are based on very low-level responses and impulses that are pre-cortical. Put another way, our stream of thought, including all the ideas that pop into your head that you act on, bubbles up from things happening in our brains that we ourselves are completely unaware of - let alone able to observe.

We don't know what made Steve Jobs the greatest tech innovator since Edison. We don't even know where our own inspirations come from. We DO know that our brains are all highly individual, very diverse - and that no one brain can do all the jobs brains do (as we've noted in our discussions of cognitive diversity). Would we imagine that machine systems based on brains would be any different, when we are only beginning to understand this reality ourselves?

My conclusion is, yes, AI is going to replace human beings in the office by the hundreds of thousands over the next five years, by the tens of millions over the next generation. A brave new world is coming. That's why it's important that we continue to think about and discuss how human beings are valued - because our labor is increasingly irrelevant.

But that doesn't mean machines can truly replace humans. They can't; there is much about human minds that is unique to human minds. AI can't get anywhere near our thoughts. Our perception, inspiration, and invention are our own; the day the machine can take them from us is far, far away. We ourselves are unable to unbox them and examine them, so deeply are they interwoven within our brains; they are safely packed away in the lovingly crafted illusions that make business and industry necessary in the first place.

Pets

Let's get this pet thing sorted out, once and for all:

Your dog would follow you over a cliff.

Your cat would eat you, if it were large enough to defeat you in combat.

The Flow of Order

There are three axes of personal emotional response underlying our social perceptions, preferences and behaviors, and one of these is to do with our innate understanding of social order.

Some people see social order as naturally vertical. Others see it as naturally horizontal.

That is, to some, social order is best when it is top-down: when there is an authority over the group that flows from above, making its way through layers that organize it for the good of the group; and to others, social order is best when the group itself decides, when the group chooses the optimum course for all and each member works to bring it about, without layers of authority.

The perpendicularity of these variations on this axis - vertical to horizontal - is, in principle, obvious: in the Authoritarian extreme, social order flows downward (God->Priest/Preacher->Husband->Wife->Children; King->Chancellor->Nobles->Commoners, etc.); in the Egalitarian extreme, people self-govern, organizing through representatives and distributing authority as evenly as possible (the Roman Republic; the US Republic, etc.). Neither of the perpendicular lines is ever completely straight, nor is any one individual an advocate for absolute conformity to rigidity in such a system (though some pretend to, in rhetoric).

The Authoritarian abhors democracy. The very idea that populations can self-govern is anathema, a dangerous proposition, even to those Authoritarians born into democratic nations. It's a sociopolitical concept that never takes root in the Authoritarian mind, because it runs counter to the concept of vertical social order that makes the Authoritarian feel safe in a dangerous world.

Thus, Authoritarians have little issue with the erosion or even the dismantling of democracy; gerrymandering or vote suppression do not seem unfair or immoral, because they are actions taken to defuse what is, in their minds, a ticking bomb. Authoritarians long for the sanctuary of a ruler's keep, and democracy can turn such rulers out with the passing of the moon.

If the United States ceases to be a democracy and truly becomes an oligarchy, the Authoritarian will not say much, and will be secretly relieved.

The Egalitarian abhors the oligarch. The notion that one voice, or one small ensemble, should decide for all is anathema, a dangerous proposition, the antithesis of democracy and freedom. Authoritarianism is the Egalitarian's worst nightmare, a path not to safety but to the greatest of dangers; it runs counter to the concept of horizontal social order that makes the Egalitarian feel empowered as a participant in society, which is by far the greater safety.

The Egalitarian takes great issue with the erosion and especially the dismantling of democracy; gerrymandering and voter suppression are ethical offenses, even crimes, against the group, worthy of severe punishment - and a ticking bomb that needs to be defused.

Put more simply, the Verticals believe the Horizontals are "destroying America"; and vice versa.

The truth is that order can never flow completely vertically or horizontally - it's simply too complex. It will always be somewhere in between. And the true social order preferences of most people are also some hybrid of vertical and horizontal, accommodating comfort zones in the mind that emerge from a complex mix of emotions and experience.

And the even deeper truth is that human beings need that hybrid mixture - our success in natural history emerged from applying different social order strategies in different circumstances, adapting so as not to die. So it was then, so it is now. Our best bet is to realize that it can never be fully one way or another, and get back to adapting...

Three Ways Moral

Michael Tomasello puts forth the observation that human beings demonstrated several distinct layers of moral development by the time we were ready to trek out of Africa.

The first (and oldest) level was a morality of Empathy. We had long since begun moving through life with a deep identification felt for those of kin and clan, an understanding that those around us were like us, inside, experiencing the same feelings, the same joys, the same fear, the same anticipations and expectations. This made what happened to those around us as important as what happened to oneself.

The second level was a morality of Fairness. If our emotions elevated our kin and clan to equality with ourselves, then what happens to me happens to you, and the impact of those happenings is shared evenly by all. We are all in this together.

The final level was a morality of Justice. An obligation to conform to common standards of behavior emerged, to ensure the propagation of the deeper moralities - systems of mores developed, habits and social mechanisms for encouraging fairness in practice.

Tomasello's work here is excellent, thoughtfully summarizing the social requirements of long-term cooperation and syncing them insightfully with what we know about the evolution of empathy and its role in our earliest group behaviors.

Now, of course, empathy is a traded commodity in our politics and economics; fairness is its fluctuation as a currency; and justice, at every level, is for sale. Capitalism has swapped out the human being for the coin, and this rock-solid system of morality that evolved over several thousand millennia has been eroded to sand in less than a hundred centuries.

Those moral impulses, however, begin in the brain, where empathy originates; that fairness impulse still flares brightly in more of us than not, and triggers a hunger and thirst for justice among the many, despite the self-interested machinations of the few.

In other words, our moral potential may be down, but it's not out. We still have, innately, all the power it once imparted, and many if not most human beings still desire it. It's a matter of putting it back to work for us as it once did. The first level, almost all of us still possess as a matter of biology; the second level, we all still apply within our in-groups - all we need do is let it continue outward. That last level - justice - is the codification of the second, and that we achieve by placing in power those who truly embrace it.

The point being - we can get back to where we once belonged.

Thought, Behavior, and AI at the Office

Intelligent thought and intelligence behavior are not the same thing. Confusing the two obfuscates the discussion of artificial intelligence on the workplace.

Intelligent thought *leads* to intelligent behavior, but it is an antecedent. Intelligent behaviors can be replicated and manipulated via variable parameters, but that's not the same as having a thought and acting on it.

This is where the argument that artificial intelligence breaks down: we can create systems that execute very complex tasks - behavior - and automate them, by setting up workflows that allow for a broad range of (changing) conditions. What we end up with looks like intelligence - but it is in fact only a product of intelligence, not intelligence itself.

Why is he telling us this?

I'm telling you this because there's a glaring reason why this isn't obvious to most people. We tend not to make the distinction between intelligent thought and behavior, because we our own behavior does *not* always derive from intelligent thought.

Too often, our behaviors follow from cues taken from others - from a leader, from our social group, from the dominant persons in our personal circle. We do as others do, think as others think, believe as others believe, without serious conscious forethought. We are all capable of putting persistent intelligent thought into our behaviors, but too often, we just run automated workflows.

If this is the best we can do, then we *can* be replaced by machines...

Lightsaber Morality

So there was a time, long, long ago, in a galaxy far, far away, when good guys and bad guys did battle with swords made of coherent light – lightsabers, they were called. And each of these good guys and bad guys had a lightsaber of a particular color.

Luke Skywalker, for instance, had a green lightsaber. But his mentor, Obi-Wan Kenobi, had a blue one.

And Darth Vader, the baddest of the bad guys, had a red one.

But here's the thing…

Red is the *least* energetic color in the visible electromagnetic spectrum, the coldest – 1.65 electron-volts; green is much more energetic, at 2.15 eV, and blue more energetic still, at 2.5.

Vader had the wimpiest blade, in other words.

Could the lightsaber colors be something else, then? A metaphor for the relative moral force of the characters?

Ant Movies and Aliens

So there was a time, long, long ago, when I made movies.

This was back in the wonder years, before digital technology, before even VHS – when a movie camera used actual film – Super 8 film – and my friends and I would make costumes and props and shoot sci-fi nonsense at the local futuristic-looking plaza.

I remember getting a new and better movie camera at one point, and taking it out for a test run to get used to its sophisticated zoom features.

I filmed some ants.

They were busily re-engineering a patch of dirt in a nearby neighborhood lot where a new house was being built, scurrying hither and yon in perfect patterns that were, after I got over my initial fascination, very predictable and even mundane. I became aware of the sameness of their paths, the sameness of their labors, the sameness – when you sum it all up – of their lives.

And then it occurred to me...

There might be aliens out there, similar to myself at the time, teenagers who liked to make movies (presumably with technology superior to Super 8 film). They might be aiming their cameras down on the earth from a high orbit, trained on us, watching us scurrying hither and yon in perfect patterns.

Four decades on, I'm far more aware of those patterns. I've been caught up in my own variations of them, all these years, and am probably as oblivious to their banality as the ants are to theirs.

Off I go each morning, from a bedroom to a bathroom down a staircase to a kitchen to a garage, then into a car and onto a road with 5,000 other cars, all marching like ants in perfect patterns, to a building with offices where others shuffle in through a common door and down a hall and into offices with near-perfect timing, proceeding to sit in chairs and face screens and go *clickity-clack* for the same number of hours, then back down halls and out doors to restaurants at feeding time - and back again, only to all leave around the same time and get in their cars and reverse their courses with precision, entering a garage and a kitchen and a bathroom and a bed.

To the alien teenager, our lives must be surging with mundane sameness of paths, sameness of labors, adding up to the very same lives.

And the patterns vary, place to place and people to people – but not by much, and not enough to strike the alien teen as truly different.

And yet…

The guy in the office next to me leads a totally different life. He has young children; mine are grown. He is active in his church; I left it behind, long ago. He is a pizza-and-beer guy, I'm a filet-and-wine guy.

The office manager leads a totally different life from either of us. She's a divorced soccer mom, good-humored and sassy, very upbeat. She sits next to the young-man-on-a-mission, our data analyst, eager and helpful, with many more years ahead of him than I have.

And so it goes, throughout the office; a shared pattern has brought our lives all together in this place, this blip on the alien teen camera, one of countless others, of no consequence more or less, to the alien – but within our shared pattern, the differences are staggering. We are leading lives that look the same from without, but are wildly diverse, within.

Is it the same for the ants? or, for that matter, for alien teens?

There's no way for me to know, of course; but I'm taking a moment to reflect on the truth that for beings like ourselves to be so much alike, and yet so different, speaks loudly and hopefully for our ultimate potential…

The Reasoning Matters

My friends and I had a real success this past week. A lengthy discussion of Intelligent Design took place, with a number of thoughtful and interesting participations, and from my point of view it was a validation of our mission here.

I and several others have posited to the group that the keys to the human future may be found in the distant human past - including the phenomenon of 'cognitive clustering,' the social concentration of many people who think the same way in the same group. This leads to atrophy of reasoning (one never has to defend one's point of view among those who agree with it) and a stagnation in the reasoning of the group overall (*we all feel this way* is reasoning enough).

But when people are de-clustered - thrown together with others who do not think in the same ways that they do - they cannot simply make a claim or state a premise and leave it at that: they must explain their thinking, conveying not just their beliefs but their process.

Our society - and, sadly, our politics - says, "The answer matters," and leaves it at that. Jerald, and hopefully our group overall, adds to that, "The reasoning matters."

And now I want to add a line, because the one thing I *didn't* get from the ID discussion that I hoped for was, "How we feel about our answer and our reasoning matters." I didn't press very hard for this, because I was enthralled by the exchanges of others. But, moving forward, I will...

Embrace Stupidity!

This may seem odd, coming from Uncle Scott - but I have to tell you, campers, I'm *tired!* Tired, deep in my bones! Tired, to the last cell of my brain!

I'm beginning to see that a life of stupidity is truly the blissful course. Consider...

To embrace stupidity is to let go of independent thought, to relinquish both the need and the responsibility for pondering things that I can now simply accept as given. Much, much less effort!

To embrace stupidity is to free up loads and loads of time - I've begun to see lately that all this time spent reading, investigating, double-checking, dialoging and questioning is flat-out *exhausting!* Can't I put all that time to better use? I haven't been to a tractor pull in well over a decade, and have yet to dive into *The Desperate Housewives of New Jersey.*

To embrace stupidity is to radically simplify so many decisions! Voting is obviously high on the list; Right and Wrong become instantly clear and Simon-simple; my place in the world is plainly marked, like a number on an auditorium chair. Life is so much less complex!

To embrace stupidity is to relax my weary grip on rationality - and science in particular, with its perpetual uncertainties, nagging tentativeness, but most of all its refusal to accommodate authority! When I cling to science, I make it impossible to cling to a leader - for science laughs at leaders, no matter their station or tenure. It is no respecter of men; when I make it my measure of truth, I can't let in the soothing song of the pack leader. Why put myself through that?

Finally, when I embrace stupidity, the stupid embrace me in return. If I rise above my stubborn addiction to knowledge and inquiry, I will be welcomed as never before by others - and into the ultimate in-group, where my tenure is assured and the affection of my peers will be boundless. My off-putting posing of awkward questions and constant uttering of illusion-bursting facts will fade away, as salt into melted butter, and I will finally revel in the social acceptance that has eluded me since childhood!

Here I stand, my choice so clear: an end to anxiety, stress, loneliness, mental exhaustion, uncertainty, and constant striving - in exchange for simplicity, relief from my worries, freedom from decisions, and the love and acceptance of great masses.

No wonder it's so popular! Who knew?

Declustering

There are many steps involved in restoring social conditions in the world that are more favorable to the workings of our social brains. Reducing the number of our trivial relationships and increasing the number of deep ones is a start; practicing eye contact in all circumstances is another; finding common purpose with those we are closest to is yet another.

But the single biggest thing we can do to strengthen ourselves and start fixing the world is to move away from cognitive clusters. Intentionally stepping back from circles of people who constantly reflect our own thoughts back to us, and finding and bonding with people who think differently enables all the other positive changes. It strengthens our own social minds while empowering the group; it calls us to utilize our innate ability to 'read' others; it forces us to clarify our goals and priorities in a way that opens up space for compromise; and it helps us to see ourselves more honestly and realistically, in relation to others.

But for the Grace of Darwin

I'll continue saying it: Our struggle is not between parties, or even ideologies: our struggle is against Authoritarianism. Parties shift frequently, ideologies evolve over time, but Authoritarianism is a primal state, a social feedback loop misplaced in time, to our seemingly eternal detriment.

The Authoritarian Leader is a narcissistic (and potentially sociopathic alpha male), unencumbered by empathy and projecting a strength and confidence that infatuates the follower. Such a leader has a knack for seeking out and mastering the reactionary buttons nested within the follower's emotions.

The Authoritarian Follower is a normal person in most respects, but has been gifted by Nature with heightened sensitivity to Threat - a boon in distant times, rejiggered for unhealthy ends by the Leader.

The Framers knew the Authoritarian Leader well, as did most Western generations from the Middle Ages onward (as did most generations from the advent of agriculture onward, really): we know this, because they explicitly built out the structure of the United States in such a way as to deny the Authoritarian any hold on the citizenry of their new nation.

They distributed power, rather than centralizing it, and did it in such a way that no single person could redistribute it; they created a lawmaking system that requires lawmakers of differing viewpoint to deliberate at length, in the implementation of their product; and they created a judicial overseer that would oscillate at a different frequency than the other branches, diluting ideological trends.

They created a system that would constrain not only the elected but the electorate, denying the tyranny of the majority.

In summary, the Framers gave us Egalitarian government in the most secure form they could conceive: government truly of, by, and for the people.

But here's where it becomes a whole new thing: in constructing this new society, the Framers were doing more than safeguarding against the Authoritarian - they were returning to our primitive roots.

The Natural Human, who once roamed the savannas of Africa in small bands, lived just as the Framers envisions - with distributed authority, an effective balance between impulse and contemplation, with power situated in no one place. How do we know? It's written into how our brains work - brains that by definition evolved, and could only have done so if they were successful, which of course they were.

We are Egalitarian by nature, as a species, if not all individually. We are beginning to understand that the Authoritarian Leader is an unintentional consequence of our social misconfiguration, and the Authoritarian Follower is simply behaving as best s/he can, given the noisy inputs the modern world offers. The rest of us - between 2/3rds and 3/4ths of the general population - are, to varying degrees, already on board with both the Framers and our Paleolithic forebears; it's a matter of locating the struggle where it truly resides.

All of this being said, it's hard not to loathe the Authoritarian, for the harm he does; it's hard not to despise his followers, for enabling him. But in the broader picture, we have the tools to prevail - the Framers saw to that. It becomes a matter of deploying them dispassionately, calmly, and with the resolve of adults responding to a crisis.

And as for our personal feelings, we must now tuck them into that place we reserve for compassion returned to the elder drifting into dementia, or sympathy for the cancer victim: this isn't about Good and Evil, this is about the constant encroaching of Nature on human minds, human bodies, human intentions. We realize that these differences that we allow to divide us and turn us against one another are natural, unavoidable, and no one's fault, and feel a glimmer of human warmth for that person across the divide - there, but for the grace of Darwin, go I...

"I have a foreboding of an America in my children's or grandchildren's time – when the United States is a service and information economy; when nearly all the key manufacturing industries have slipped away to other countries; when awesome technological power are in the hands of a very few, and no one representing the public interest can even grasp the issues; when the people have lost the ability to set their own agendas or knowledgeably question those in authority; when, clutching our crystals and nervously consulting our horoscopes, our critical faculties in decline, unable to distinguish between what feels good and what's true, we slide, almost without noticing, back into superstition and darkness."

~Carl Sagan

Patriarchal Morality

Patriarchies are ultimately about control, pushing beyond social organization to the manipulation of individual behavior in the course of redirecting personal goals and objectives to satisfy an authoritarian requirement. This extends from pacification of social challengers thru governance of expectation to controlling the sexuality and reproductive behaviors of females. Entire societies and cultures are sculpted by a patriarchy's manipulative ideals for carving down its constituents to its behavioral ideals.

Patriarchy is the heart of authoritarianism, the notion that the male parent is (and should be) in charge of the female parent and all the offspring. This is social dominance behavior, pushing combat between males deeper into the tribe's social structure. It is chimpanzee behavior, and aberrant in homo sapiens, and very rarely seen in primates in general; most primates are peaceful, and the chimpanzee's exception owes to environmental circumstance that both the bonobo and hominin avoided. There is no developmental benefit to humans in behaving like chimpanzees, and potential for overwhelming harm - which we have been suffering for upwards of 12,000 years now.

Patriarchal moralities are so socially unsupportable and so instinctually resistance-worthy in humans that they can only be implemented through fantastic means - the construction of invented threats and mystical consequences for their violation. People of both genders tend to resist, to circumvent and transcend the patriarchal will by any means available; thus we have millennia of tug-of-war behind us, with patriarchal social order weighing down on countless human lives, as those weighed-down participants have lived under the radar - loving the wrong people, pushing back privately against sanctioned unfairness and inequalities, privately resenting circumstances that minimize and demean us for the dice-rolls of birth.

I note in the earlier discussion that it is difficult to get others to even consider that this is not how things have always been, and definitely not how things should be; but so entrenched is patriarchy in the human social frame that we seldom get a glimpse of anything better (though the science fiction genre has worked overtime to provide one). We have a hard time getting past what we've seen and been told all our lives, in order to ponder what might be better.

I suggest that this is our starting point. Step One in bringing about change is imagining what that change might be. As humankind continues to evolve, and patriarchy fades in utility (even for the patriarchs), what will arise? Each possibility invites its own deep discussion: an end to inequality; a renaissance of individual human potential; a cessation of social manipulation; the elevation of woman to her rightful position in the human story; and the restoration of common vision.

How do those sound?

My Superhero Identity

So I'm having this superhero conversation with a kid, asking him - if he had powers, would he rather be an Avenger or in the Justice League? And we start talking about what powers we'd like to have.

I would want my superhero name to be Plato, and my superpower would be rhetoric. Tony Stark would be in the sky with Vision and Thor, holding back the alien hordes of Thanos, and he would call down to me, "Some of them are breaking through! Plato, it's up to you!"

And I would stand firm against them, lift my hand to the sky and cry, "Duty! Sublime and mighty name that embraces nothing charming or insinuating but requires submission, and yet does not seek to move the will by threatening anything that would arouse natural aversion or terror in the mind but only holds forth a law that of itself finds entry into the mind and yet gains reluctant reverence (though not always obedience), a law before which all inclinations are dumb, even though they secretly work against it; what origin is there worthy of you, and where is to be found the root of your noble descent which proudly rejects all kinship with the inclinations, descent from which is the indispensable condition of that worth which human beings alone can give themselves?"

And they would fall from the sky, stunned into - you know - contemplation...

Chintzy

Whatever happened to the word *chintzy*? That's a word you just never hear anymore. People used to say, 'He's really *chintzy*,' or, 'Wow, how *chintzy* can you get?' We haven't heard talk like that in decades! My iPhone even rebels against the word. *Chintzy* is on the verge of extinction.

I'm just sayin'.

Guns and Brains

Another mass shooting – Las Vegas, this time, and it marks a new record in US gun massacres. This is a big, big subject, one that interweaves itself into other big, big subjects. There is no easy answer, and the objective frame available to us in pursuing its analysis is unsatisfying, because it can't absorb the emotions that this subject stirs.

I have an essay, "Yoga Pants, Bullets, and Coins" that highlights the human tendency to invent artifacts that become cognitive shortcuts in our heads - truncations of mental processes that simplify and accelerate our responses and activities, but which cause us to substitute the shortcut - intended to simplify our burden of thought - for thought itself.

Guns stand out here. Though very new in human history - can you believe that it's only since our grandparents' grandparents' time that you can fire more than once without reloading? - they have rapidly become so ubiquitous as to seem like a human appendage. But no matter how familiar, they will never cease to be what they are: a simplification of the taking of human life. As Larry Niven summed it up - "Point at a man, make a fist - he dies."

This takes all the cognitive burden and physical complexity out of killing another. If all I have is my bare hands, the proposition of life-taking is much more complex: the risk to me is far, far greater, so significant planning comes into play. If I have tools other than my hands, the risk is less, but the planning becomes more complex still. With a gun, all these burdens vanish.

This is one of many human innovations that become problematic, when fully pondered - a convenience that undermines the thought that should be part of the process it impacts. That problem alone calls us to scrutiny.

But, of course, the gun issue is still more complicated: those who rally around the right to possess guns are not focused on easing the strain of killing - they call up their right to defend themselves.

Now we're into *very* deep cognitive waters, because the impulse to self-defend is far, far stronger and far more prevalent than the impulse to take another's life. The gun issue has stretched the full spectrum of the brain, from our most philosophical ponderings to our deepest and most hair-trigger fears.

I can't address that full spectrum in a single pass, but I can make note of a few things:

- The people who control this debate include the less-than-1% who are part of the gun lobby, on the one side, and an equally minute counterpart on the other side who would have all guns banned. In the middle - 98% of us, who have no problem with guns in principle but would like to see some adult supervision of their use.

- So deep is our emotional connection to the issue itself - discussion of devices which instantly end a human life - that our powers of reason go out the window when discussing it.

- So personal is our conceptualization of the use of a gun that it overwrites our conceptualizations of community, nation, and government - we have difficulty maintaining a broad perspective when we talk about life and death, one-on-one.

- This issue stirs fears and unease within as individuals to the degree that we are inclined to cling too fiercely to our own thoughts about it, and have a great deal of trouble putting it out on a larger table for examination.

It's easy to knock these things down, perched high above them: the Second Amendment isn't about personal gun ownership to begin with, it's about the government provisioning for defense of itself - militias repel invaders, they are not police forces - and "well-regulated" means "well-regulated," not "utterly un-regulated." It is astonishing that this issue is so paralyzing that those words literally get rewritten in the mind.

The notion that gun ownership is about defending one's home against a tyrannical government is likewise an easy target, from high above: there's the *Star Trek* episode where a peaceful distant colony faces invasion, and hunkers down with their pistols and rifles to repel the invaders, their fear so amputating their reasoning that the Starfleet hero of the story must take out their water supply with a single shot from a single weapon to get their attention long enough to say, "They don't have to come down here and shoot you - they can bomb you into oblivion from orbit." So can the US military. It is so obvious that Citizen Joe and his three weapons and shoebox supply of ammo can be taken out with an RPG or two from the safety of an armored vehicle down the block that one does not feel the need to point out all the missing reasoning - or the fact that the same people who say their guns are a defense against their own government are the same people who feel the US military needs another $60 billion or so this coming year, because it's so under-fed.

And that's before we get to the demonstrable falsehood that Obama or Hillary or the Left is "coming for your guns!" By the numbers and by his record, Obama is (shamefully) the most gun-friendly president in recent memory. The objective truth is that most of the Left and most of the Right are fine with guns, and guns aren't going away anytime soon - adults just want to see adult rules in place. Period. *No one* is coming for your guns.

No, this is all about something much deeper.

We have, many times, pointed out that each of us is born with a brain that is somewhat different from other brains - and that we will enter the world, day by day, with a point of view that is inevitably not the same as our neighbor's. That doesn't make anyone of us more right or wrong than any other. It just makes us different.

When it comes to the gun issue, we realize that we each think of threat to ourselves and our families in different ways - and that some of us are more willing to embrace the risk of trusting our neighbor or our society or our government than others. We come by this variation very naturally - and its existence is a species-saving trait.

I have fired weapons. I was an ROTC cadet. But I have never owned a gun and have no interest in ever owning a gun. I think they're silly. I have no illusions about my neighbor or my government. And I don't think I am living my life in an unreasonably risky way. The truth is, I live in a peaceful, friendly neighborhood and almost never even lock my front door.

On the other hand, that's just my own experience. I have friends who have been in combat. I know three people well who suffer from PTSD. I know people who own guns who have never fired them, simply because the presence of the gun makes them feel safer. And when I was young, a young boy in our church shot himself in the spleen and almost died, because he found his dad's pistol. The point being, there are many perspectives, pro and con, good and bad, that transcend my own, so it's pointless for me to parade my own point of view. The Second Amendment never even makes it to the party in this debate, and if it did, it wouldn't be relevant.

The gun control debate is about emotions that have little to do with our government and the society we live in - and the deeper issue gets circumvented, because of those emotions.

The deeper issue is that a vanishingly-small minority is completely controlling a dialog that very much needs to proceed – drowning out many voices that need to be heard - and the consequences of that stalled dialog spill out of our televisions and our RSS feeds all too perpetually these days. Let's reassert the voices of those 98% in the middle who just want that reasonable discussion, and then see where we are...

Like-mindedness

Like-mindedness is emotionally pleasing.

Like-mindedness is deeply reassuring.

Like-mindedness is a profoundly powerful social bond.

It replaces the burden of reason.

It relaxes the need for justification.

It weakens the thinking of its indulgents.

It sharply reduces the decision-making capacity of groups it forms around.

It creates false and empty social distinctions between individuals and groups.

It inculcates a false sense of superiority.

It leads to deep and pervasive error in thought and behavior.

It leads to social inequality.

It stunts self-assessment and the honest assessment of others.

It justifies the worst of human behaviors, from misogyny to bigotry to war.

It inspires competition for its own sake, usurping our empathies.

It replaces, disruptively and ineffectively, all the cognitive advantages that truly empower human beings, from contemplation to mutual awareness to altruistic reciprocity.

It has weakened us as a species, rending our capacity for collective unanimity, and taken us to the edge of ruin. It is, unchecked, our clearest path to extinction.

Our Daily Dunbar

Recapturing the social dynamics of our Paleolithic origins – that expansive stretch of millennia when we, Homo sapiens, the universe's ultimate cooperators, were at our thriving best – involves a number of serious commitments.

The first is the commitment to perpetual togetherness. Social groups in prehistory weren't online chat groups, gangs that met for drinks after work or clubs one attended once a week; they were groups that literally spent most of the hours of the day together.

The second is the commitment to common purpose. Social groups back then were not organized around their favorite music or sports team or preferred deity; they were focused on surviving. Their day-to-day shared purpose – living - bound them together inextricably, giving them a common agenda that defined their thoughts, actions, plans and successes.

The third is the commitment to cognitive diversity. Ancient social groups made it through all those centuries of centuries, emerging not only alive but much stronger, because of the richness of their differences; though they had no way to be conscious of it, that diversity equipped them to handle *any* problem, no matter how big, no matter how complex, no matter how imminent.

These three features – combined with a passive observance of the Dunbar Limit (that cap on group size that kept human tribes within their optimum cognitive capacity) – represent the keys to human group success. They define human cooperation as natural selection refined it, the conditions under which we can, together, achieve peak performance. Before the dawn of civilization, such groups took down mammoths with sticks and stones – something that's hard to imagine of social groups today.

Our overpopulated, over-segmented society deprives us of *all* of these strengths.

We are isolated more often and more deeply, by orders of magnitude, than our distant parents; our destinies are only passively intertwined, at least in our own minds, to the point that few work together for any goals but their own; and our diversity of mind is lost, as our great numbers make it possible for us to surround ourselves with echoes of our own thoughts and words. Strong enough to break the world though we may be, we are at our core weaker than we have ever been, as a species.

How do we get back? Where can Dunbar groups be built, within this uneven world we've created? Not our churches; they exist specifically for cognitive clustering, not cognitive diversity (and the same is true of our political tribes). Not our fan enclaves; though often diverse and socially positive, they present no common purpose of consequence. Not our social networks; even when they are cognitively diverse (seldom) and unified in theme (often), they don't offer authentic fellowship.

Where, then? I submit that most of us participate in a potential Dunbar environment most every day: our workplace.

When we commit to a job, we are committing to a purpose, one that can only be achieved through group cooperation. We commit to spending more time, day by day, with our working colleagues than we typically spend with our own family. And, though there are a few exceptions, most workplaces do not actively select for cognitive type: it is likely that your workplace includes both liberals and conservatives, the religious and the not, some egalitarians, some libertines, a few creative types and some worker bees, people who are bold and people who are timid, and an authoritarian or two. Most workplaces are not only cognitively randomized, but cognitively rich.

In short, most workplaces include the basic ingredients of a successful Paleolithic tribe – something that can't be said for the nuclear family, churches, or political parties.

Though our hierarchical, authoritarian business traditions dampen it, there is a pervasive potential within almost every workplace to solve any problem, for almost every work environment contains numerous members of every problem-solving type. Though our economic system discourages the even distribution of the wealth of business success, there is the clear potential for every member within the workplace to commit to the mission and purpose of the enterprise.

And the togetherness is built in: we spend more hours per week with our colleagues, on average, than we do with our spouses and children, by far. Here, it's our culture that discourages the depth of social connection that could lift the workplace to Dunbar status, but we've all experienced at least bits of it: that friendship, born at the office, that becomes fulfilling and supportive, extending for years beyond the point that one or both have moved on; that mentoring relationship that eventually transcends work skills and inspiration, becoming almost familial; that shared intimacy that starts out with daily chats and winds up on speed dial.

The ingredients of the Dunbar group, with all its potential for success, cognitive benefits and deep social rewards, is right there in our daily trek to work. And the upside is formidable: pursuing the Dunbar ideals within such a familiar and comfortable setting is empowering to the organization and individual alike, resulting in collective accomplishment and personal growth.

And the path from here to there isn't as intimidating as one might think. It is, in fact, pretty simple.

Make a daily effort to really know and understand your colleagues better; engage people in conversation daily, and not just the ones you are naturally friendly with – all of them. Take a genuine interest in their lives, and take advantage of every opportunity to work more closely with them.

Study more deeply your organization's goals and objectives, and where you can, invest emotional energy in committing to those goals and objectives. We don't have to buy in all the way; we only need to find something to care about beyond our paycheck.

Finally, bring the best of your own thinking to the table, speaking out in whatever way works for you, while simultaneously seeking out and really hearing points of view other than your own. Understand that your organization is stronger precisely because there are many points of view.

Challenge those you don't agree with, but also be welcoming and encouraging of them for their own sake. While urging yourself to speak out, encourage others to do the same, even (especially) those who might view you as an opponent.

If all of this seems preachy, well, perhaps it is, and I guess that's inevitable. But I'd argue that these are baby steps that carry us many miles. Taking them is a personal thing, requiring no consensus, and we've already underscored the rewards. We can also find no downside: even if we move this direction and fail to change the world, those who go there will experience enhanced awareness, greater on-the-job success, and stronger in-house relationships. And if we take down a mammoth or two along the way, all the better.

Bringing Back the Stone Age

In 1996 I wrote a novel about a Bill Gates-like nerd billionaire who crashes in the Rockies with six of his entourage and the pilot of their twin-prop plane. Lost, and feared dead by the frantically-searching outside world, the party of eight fights to survive and return to civilization during a heart-stopping five-day crisis. To make this all the more interesting, I had my Gates party turn completely upside down, in terms of their relative value to one another, their social usefulness, and most importantly their ultimate survival value – inverting their social structure so that the Gates figure lost all authority, and the *pilot* became the leader of the group. This made the story much more fun, and much more worth telling.

What was the point? *That's who we really are* – the people we become when our survival is no longer a given, our mutual dependency no longer an abstraction – the people we were 10,000 years ago, 25,000 years ago, before agriculture and civilization made it possible for us to manipulate the world around us – and each other.

I called that book *The Stone Age*, for obvious reasons, and what I hoped to convey was the true antiquity of our minds, and how it bubbles to the surface when we are threatened. But I wasn't just saying we carry ancient baggage around in our brains.

In our brains, today, *it is still the Stone Age*. Our neural circuitry is still much what it was then. Think about that! We are navigating through a world unimagined in our grandparents' time, or our great-great-great grandparents' time, a world that hovers between Rod Serling Scary and *Star Trek* Awesome – which we created! – bursting with complexities of our own making, fantasies challenging the far borders of the Absurd, a world fraught with dangers which no human brain has ever conceived, *let alone been wired for*.

And we are wandering through this super-attenuated, energy-drunk, digital fantasia armed only with a lump of protein that is fine-tuned for noticing and remembering weather patterns, following animals in the woods, and grasping that stones can become liquids, and back again. We have just barely, *barely* generated the optimal neurochemical balance for raising crops successfully, year after year, remembering more than one password, and setting up series recording on our DVRs.

But, you protest loudly and immediately, *we have stepped beyond our atmosphere! We have walked on a world not our own! We control the lightning, and are mastering the atom! We can feed hundreds of millions, and write sonnets and symphonies, and splice our own genes!!! We have Twain, we have Vonnegut, we have Hitchens and Lady Gaga! We are packing for Mars! GEEZUS! WE HAVE SIDE 2 OF ABBEY ROAD!!!*

All true. I grant every point and could add to the list myself all day long. But *why* do we have these things, our brains being what they are? And the answer is, because – like Newton – *we stand on the shoulders of giants.* Each of us inherits all the knowledge and experience of previous generations, and as we roll forward, that is building to a tsunami of intellectual treasure. But …

It is only a handful of generations of true substance we want to carry forward … the wonder experienced by our parents' great-grandparents' great-grandparents … before which, education was denied to the masses, science was done in shadows, and our teenage daughters were burned as witches by Evangelical congregations, impatient for their picnics.

It is a mere 30 generations since Henry II consolidated England, advancing the nation-state; a mere 75 since Jesus opened the first Long John Silver's; a mere 130 since humans learned to smelt iron, and less than 200 since we learned to mix copper and tin to make bronze.

Sticks and stones? *We were still doing that only 250 grandpaws ago,* when we first figured out how to build houses with wood – 70 grandpaws after we figured out how to make bricks stick together.

I'm sure to be saying an unpopular thing, pointing out that our gray matter is only of Flintstones quality. And many may be resisting the idea, because we clearly are living much higher and finer than Fred and Wilma and Pebbles.

So let's think about it … How many Facebook friends do you have? 300? 500? 1,000?

Take an hour, take two, and off the top of your head, send me an email describing *every last one of them in detail.*

Here are the phone numbers of my youth: (606) 277-8483, (606) 278-8434, (404) 344-7477, (317) 362-4072, (502) 695-4452. And one more: (812) 945-6457. Read that line *once,* close your eyes, then *call the last number and recite from memory all the others.*

You can't do it. Why? *Because your brain isn't wired to handle that level of detail. Why not? Because your survival doesn't depend on it.*

Your brain is wired to remember *the brothers and sisters of the tribe your great(x300)-grandparents lived and died among* ... it is programmed to parse *the details of the past week* ... to favor the scent of *three or four members of the opposite sex,* whose immune systems are genetically optimal for reproducing with your own ... for following *six or seven trail markers away from and back to the group.*

Those capabilities were honed and sharpened, not over dozens of generations of men and women like ourselves, but *thousands* ... about 5,000, possibly more. They are precious talents, thankfully written into the fabric of our cells, beacons in our destiny for near-infinite nights and seasons, on our perilous path to the sewing of animal hides for warmth, the invention of writing, and tuning in to *Jersey Shore.*

My take-home point: when we see behaviors based on these ancient, tried-and-true genetic influences, which allowed our great(x300)-grandparents to survive and thrive in the World Before Cornfields and Sanitation, we shouldn't be surprised; Those Who Believe in Evolution are so quick to taunt Those Who Don't that they forget that *evolution takes millennia to effect true genetic change.*

Why is he telling us this?

I'm telling you this because we are currently inundated with Bronze Age thinking, in our modern social milieu, on the Internet, in our politics, in our religious discourse. It is epidemic in scope.

It would be ridiculous to deny it: we have contemporary policy makers, citizens exposed to the accumulated knowledge of the entire

Enlightenment, *struggling with all their might to reduce the women around them to mere property.* We have, staggeringly – breathtakingly – contemporary women, wives and mothers, willing to accept that status! We have societies (the United States in particular), built upon the abstracted concept that skin color and historical background and linguistic nuance (ancient flags of geographical competition for resources) are inconsequential, on the verge of catastrophic collapse – because *persons of differing skin color have acquired alpha status.*

Do these things seem ridiculous, even Neanderthal, to the modern mind? Of course they do. But they are *natural conclusions*, because the 'modern mind' has the leg-up of vastly-accelerated social transmission of knowledge – which is transmitted, or not, based on a genetically-determined neural receptivity that is not under the receiver's control.

It is entirely to do with the level of dopamine receptivity that exists within the Eye of the Beholder, and the social training (i.e., parental discipline) that the EB experiences within the first five years of life. It is a spectrum.

Some people can override the neurological impulses of our ancient past, based on abstracted, socially-transmitted information … and some cannot. And whether or not they can, or cannot, *is not up to them*; it is written (genetically) into their personal neurology, and reinforced (or not) by Nurture.

Why is he telling us that?

I'm telling you that because I wake up to a daily Internet diet of enlightened, informed rancor toward the Bronze Age Thinkers for their addle-minded devotion to Literary Literalism ("the Holy Bible doesn't mean a thing if it isn't an encyclopedia!"), purely neurophysiological patriarchy ("Women are subordinate to men, because men are smarter and stronger – Jehovah says so!"), and Stone Age (forget the Bronze Age!) impulses to explain the thunder and lightning ("Christ is returning, the world will be destroyed by fire and Believers will be taken up!").

And even this isn't news, to people who actually think, and read books. So why am I taking a couple of hours out of my schedule, on a holiday, to write this?

Because many of my Internet friends, enlightened and educated and liberated from the social shackles of Bronze-Age memes, tirelessly shout down the Bronze-Age thinkers, with the accusation, "Bronze Age thinking! Bronze Age thinking!"

… and it's time someone spoke up, and said, "Bronze Age thinking may hold us back … it may be out of date … it may be useless and destructive … but *it's natural*. Those who think in such ways do so *because it is natural for them to do so*, and it was reinforced by their upbringing — at the hands of others who naturally embodied such thinking."

Does it need to stop? *Yes. Bronze Age thinking is inappropriate in the socio-political environment we have created.* On the other hand, not everyone is aware of this frame, or these impulses, or the scientific explication of them that informs our awareness – not by a long shot. Why not? Because our sensitivity to the impulses of our past, in the direction of Group Fealty (dedication to common effort for group survival) or Novelty-Seeking Efficiency (the ability to track and capture game – nutrition – for the survival of the tribe) fall into a neurochemical spectrum we inherit – not of our making.

Every day, my Internet friends berate their neurologically variant siblings for their Neanderthal thinking, their "Bronze Age" beliefs, their un-enlightened awareness. *And they are right to do so, from the standpoint of human progress.* And I'm with them, in principle. But I have to account for their awareness of what's driving this, and why.

If you're going to swear fealty to Science and Empiricism, by all means, do so! But you are lashing out at the Bronze Agers on emotional grounds, not empirical grounds, and there's not much point to that.

Those who endlessly say deplorable things about Others, those who are *black! brown! Hispanic! female!* and so on, do not do so because they are stupid, or uninformed, or hateful … but because their nervous systems are (like yours) *40,000 years out of sync,* and they did not receive the genetic blessing of low dopamine sensitivity (and, possibly) rearing by parents with low dopamine sensitivity that you did.

I'm saying that we can't have it both ways.

Either we give our loyalty to science and objective observation, which tells us clearly that our tribal impulses are genetic and outdated and perpetuated by our social rules for rearing of the young (with all of those neurological implications) — or we don't, and we capitulate to an unreasoned mirror of the irrationality of the genetically-driven, neurologically-predetermined conflicts of The Stone Age.

Which will it be? Are we enlightened, or aren't we?

It would be incredibly convenient, and species-supporting, and enlightened, and generally advantageous in responsibly exploiting the natural world, if our genetic proclivities, honed by thousands of years of confrontation with the environment, happened to align with our abstractions of what we've seen and thought about, where that natural environment is concerned. It would be to the overwhelming advantage of the babies we create, and the partners we choose, and cherish, and love – regardless of their color or their geographic origin or their personal characteristics – if we were neurologically capable of handling the abstracted variables that define them, over and above those additional variables presented by Others that we encounter, day to day — over and above our water coolers, singles bars, cell phones, text limits, and eHarmony and Match.com.

But that turns out not to be the case …

Discovery

A week from now, a new *Star Trek* TV series will debut. It will be the sixth such series in 50 years (not counting the 1973 cartoon version).

As a life-long fan, I can't help but be filled with anticipation – but like most fans, I'm also somewhat apprehensive. There has been lots and lots of *Trek* over the years (more than *Star Wars*, more than Superman and Batman and Spider-Man, even more than Doctor Who), and we'd be less than honest if we didn't admit that the *Trek* we've been given over the decades has been hit-and-miss.

Star Trek, you see, differs from the others in an important, even essential way: it isn't just good guys and bad guys or cool future tech or nerdy adventure. *Star Trek* is about an idea, and it's an idea that's up there with the greatest human thought and literature – the idea that humankind, without help from gods or "destiny" or some Jesus-Saves Force will prevail on our own, and create a future that is positive, uplifting, and packed with endless potential. Its central message is that the human race will not only survive but thrive, eventually reaching for the stars, and in doing so we will leave our disheartening legacy of greed, hatred, mistrust and violence behind us, once and for all.

This new show is called *Star Trek: Discovery*, and I submit that this is the best subtitle imaginable for a *Trek* series. The path to that marvelous future imagined by series creator Gene Roddenberry is, inevitably, a journey of discovery, first and foremost– a journey into unknowns that are about more than just survival, but a quest for growth and enrichment of a deeper kind.

Humanism sums up Roddenberry's *Trek* mantra, and humanism it certainly is, borrowed from his sci-fi pal Isaac Asimov, one of the movement's most prominent proponents. The more Roddenberry explored it, the more committed he became to it, and the more he insisted that *Trek* reflect it, to the point of forbidding conflict between the principal characters of *Star Trek: The Next Generation*. This made life difficult for series writers, but it also made *Trek* stand out on a sci-fi horizon populated primarily by survival-of-the-fittest and dystopian angst.

But the implementation of Roddenberry's vision was spotty, at best. Writer-director Nicholas Meyer, for instance (who delivered *Star Trek II: The Wrath of Khan*, the most acclaimed of the original cast movies), based one of his films[1] on the premise that the original Enterprise officers were essentially racists, regarding Klingons with all the racial sensitivity of David Duke. The racial loathing was multidirectional: Vulcans are pretty racist themselves, it turns out, as seen in both the prequel series *Enterprise* and in the first of the *Trek* reboot films. And while there is little greed to be found in a universe where energy flows freely and material needs are universally met, there is very nearly as much aggression and shooting and things blowing up in *Star Trek* as there is in *Star Wars*.

What can we expect? We want to expect exactly what the title promises: Discovery. A series about a Federation starship with a diverse crew, venturing out into the unknown – not for wealth or conquest, but for knowledge and experience. The show takes place about a decade before the adventures of the original Enterprise – that is, in the mid-22nd century – at a time when relations between the Federation and its neighbors were still tentative, so there is potential for constructive conflict.

And what we've seen of the crew is certainly diverse: a female captain, white and black and Asian actors populating the roles, aliens among the crew, a gay crewmember, even Spock's father. Lots to work with. And there's even Harry Mudd as a recurring character, to give us a baseline of comparison for measuring humanity's improvement.

We may or may not get the *Trek* series we've been waiting for this past decade. J.J. Abrams' three reboot movies gave us much of what we love, but they were more adventure than discovery, more guns than minds. The toss-up comes down to an interesting circumstance in the show's production: Gene Roddenberry's son Rod is an executive producer, and will certainly be guardian to his father's vision. And the show's head writer-producer is… none other than Nick Meyer, who explicitly rejects that vision.

---

[1] *Star Trek VI: The Undiscovered Country*, 1991. The Klingon Empire, facing economic collapse, turns to the Federation for support, through a progressive chancellor. Assigned to escort him to a summit, Kirk and crew are drawn into political intrigue, and in the process let their barely-disguised loathing of Klingons hang out. This slip into 20th-century thinking was deeply troubling to the dying Roddenberry, who made his displeasure known to Meyer only weeks before he passed. Meyer, a disciple of both Shakespeare and Dickens, is the most intellectually sophisticated writer-director in the Star Trek fold – but not persuaded of the potential for human perfectibility.

Ex astris, scientia – "From the stars, knowledge" – is Starfleet's motto, and it couldn't be more perfect. Can a *Trek* series that truly lives up to its title – a series about Discovery, and not just the starship – be exciting, compelling, even moving, without lots of space battles and animosities? Will it be worth our time? Or will they bungle it out of the gate?

I'm holding out for the former. I'm hoping for a show that explores not just the final frontier, but the inner discoveries that happen when new life is encountered and we must be willing to change, if we hope to coexist with it. I'm hoping for a show about ideas, where the conflict is in wrestling with challenging thoughts and difficult problems, rather than which ship's shields will hold out the longest.

Star Trek is 51 years old, and its father is now 26 years dead. I'm hoping for a show that echoes his most steadfast assurance, conveyed through his creation: that the human adventure is just beginning…

The Smell of the Lord

So I'm walking into a Baptist church in the Midwest for a wedding, and I hold the door for the maid of honor.

As I step inside, I'm hit with that wave of familiarity that remains fresh in my memories, even though I haven't set foot in a church in ages. It's a wave of recall, of stubborn ambience, of uninvited memory – an insistent cord that snaps me back to my abandoned past like the elastic band on a paddleball.

"All churches smell the same," I suddenly realize – and I wonder why this has never registered before.

The maid of honor pauses and turns to me.

"All churches smell the same," she says in a low voice, as if Yahweh Himself were in the room and she'd just asked, 'Who farted?' She's right, of course.

Suddenly I'm five years old again, descending into a cinderblock basement painted the yellow of children's construction paper, leaving behind the sanctuary, with its vision-confounding windows and hard-as-stone, stained-oak pews and their puffy thin-carpet padding. Florescent light beckons. There's a fellowship hall with long, collapsible tables and Army-brown folding chairs around here somewhere, filled with fried chicken and covered-dish corn and green beans and scalloped potatoes and styrofoam cups full of lemonade and iced tea, and the scent of coffee emanating from large metal cylinders somewhere nearby.

"They do!" I quietly agree.

She looks me in the eye. "It's the smell of the Lord," she states emphatically. I nod. She's right, of course.

I've known this smell all my life. It is, indeed, the smell of the Lord – the unmistakable aroma of righteousness, olfactory evidence of piety and salvation. My father, an evangelical pastor, gave my siblings and me generous exposure to so many of these ample bunkers in our youth. My memory tells no word of lie: they do, indeed, all smell *exactly* the same.

But I'm knocked off kilter by a revelation: this is a *Baptist* church, and I'm a Campbellite! (a spun-off Church-of-Christer). I'm suddenly aware that over the years I've been in so many of God's houses – Church of Christ, Baptist, Methodist, Lutheran, you name it – and the non-denominational scent of the divine holds true, across the deepest of doctrinal divides.

Another few moments of thought, and my awe deepens: for I have played weddings on pipe organs in Catholic domiciles, and there, too - that holy aroma! This most ecumenical of odors arises in cathedrals, temples, sanctuaries of all creed (though I confess I've never been in a mosque) - hanging like a yellow sign in the rear window of the day, announcing "Deity on Board".

As guests are parsed Bride and Groom in the sanctuary, I ruminate - this is not an isolated phenomenon. Consider, for instance, the following:

- All government buildings smell the same;
- All old theaters smell the same;
- All high school gymnasiums smell the same;

…and yet they all smell very distinct; you could be blindfolded and escorted into any of them, and you'd identify your surroundings in a heartbeat – but none of them smell like *this*.

There's something primal at work here, I think. In nature – and, by extension, the wayback past – the smell of a place gave us as much or more information about it than our vision and touch, a distinct survival advantage. Even on approach, the scent of a stream or the edge of a wood or the mouth of a cave would say, "Feces!" or "Large animals died here!" or "Hungry predators await!" – and a Go/No-Go would click in the mind. So it is with all of the above.

The government building is made of metal doors and tile bathrooms and stucco walls and ceilings. Old theaters smell of crushed velvet and the oil of hinged chairs and stale popcorn. High school gymnasiums are the maple of the court floor and the sweaty, jock-strappy reek of youth.

And the Smell of the Lord is aged oak and frequently-vacuumed carpet and fabric covering everything, with the must of the occasional heavy drape and fleeting wisps of crayon.

The Lord's scent might signal hellfire or haven; it might accompany authoritarian exclusivism or Unitarian tolerance, the justification of the mighty or sanctuary for the downtrodden. It might herald the intimidating waft of legalist reprobation or the honey-sweet welcome of egalitarian quittance – the dull thump of tribe, or the whistling winds of amnesty.

Only one thing is certain: that smell is the one damn thing, the *only*damnthing about houses of worship that is, between them, even remotely consistent.

"Modern man has been alienated from himself, from his fellow men, and from nature. He has been transformed into a commodity, experiences his life forces as an investment which must bring him the maximum profit obtainable under existing market conditions. Human relations are essentially those of alienated automatons, each basing his security on staying close to the herd, and not being different in thought, feeling, or action. While everybody tries to be as close as possible to the rest, everybody remains utterly alone, pervaded by the deep sense of insecurity, anxiety and guilt which always results when human separateness cannot be overcome."

~Erich Fromm, *The Art of Loving*

Mommy and Daddy and Erich Fromm

The philosopher/linguist George Lakoff has put forth a number of insightful and challenging conceptualizations of how humans mobilize their sociopolitical bias in the world, and his most useful is the Strict Father/Nurturant Parent Model.

This model holds that conservatives, or those we see on the political Right, hold to a 'Strict Father' morality frame – a social filter that remaps the social universe into a top-down hierarchy, with 'Father' on top, layers of Father proxies in between, with mom and the kids on the bottom. From this structure, Lakoff points out, all Authoritarian social order can be derived: in religion, it's God->Priest/Preacher->Dad->Mom->Kids; in government, it's King->Chancellor->Nobles->Commoners. Moral 'goodness', in this frame, follows from the edicts of whoever's on top (be it God or Donald Trump) and how strictly those edicts are adhered to; obedience is achieved by that childhood mechanism 'Punishment/Reward'; and 'evil' is deviation from that order.

The other half of the model, the Nurturant Parent side, is the political Left's preference: a social filter that remaps the social universe laterally, rather than top-down, with no one on top and no oneon the 'bottom'. From this structure, Lakoff demonstrates, all Egalitarian social order can be derived: authority is dispensed via the consensus of the group, rather than by class, and all members have equal access to the 'nurture' society provides. The order, then, is Group Consensus->Assigned Leader->Group, and Father is replaced by Parent – both being equal, gender aside – with moral 'goodness' deriving from the well-being of the group, and obedience achieved by example, rather than by force... with 'evil' being the subversion of the well-being of the group.

Lakoff, being a political activist on the Left, favors the Nurturant Parent frame, and to be sure, that's the frame we see most clearly in early human prehistory, based on what we know so far: primate communities that follow this frame are far more socially successful that those that do not (*pan paniscus* v. *pan troglodyte*). *Both* of these frames (as well as several others) are essential to the human story, so we'll set

Lakoff aside at this point, and turn to another important voice: Dr. Erich Fromm, the venerated German psychoanalyst who launched our investigation of Authoritarianism in the early years of World War II, who has much to say about the psychosocial impact of parents.

In his 1956 masterpiece *The Art of Loving*, Fromm masterfully analyzes the effects of Western civilization (and Capitalism in particular) upon the human capacity for love, cooperation, and mutual understanding. In particular, he deep-dives into the innate features of the parent-child connection, and how those natural feelings, actions and responses wind up corrupted and toxic in the Western social frame.

The essence of Fromm's thesis is that Western civilization (and Capitalism in particular) heavily revises the roles of all its members – and does quite a number on father, mother, and child, in particular. Per Fromm, *I love because I am loved* is the natural reality of the infant, responding to the constant care and unconditional affection of mother, father, and tribe, in our pre-civilization setting – a reality that matures into *I am loved because I love*, with respect not just to mother and father but to the entire tribe, as the child grows, surrounded by the constant reciprocity of intimacy and support provided by the group.

We don't live that way in Western society, of course; our model for existence is constant consumption and exchange, wherein all the elements of life – including human beings themselves – are traded commodities. The modern human is no longer *loved because s/he loves* - s/he is loved because she trades for the commodity of love.

And this occurs because of the bifurcation of parental roles in the modern world, says Fromm: the unconditional love expressed to the infant dissipates over time, particularly in fathers, who are now territorial and commodity-driven; the objects of the world are now possessions to be discriminately disbursed. Paternal love is now conditional, rather than unconditional: *I love you because you fulfill my expectations, because you do your duty, because you are like me*, as Fromm describes it.

More broadly, love in the age of commodities is no longer a universal expression of the individual, an offering to the whole of his/her existence, but an object-oriented thing, assigned to this object but not that one, doled out like coins from a purse when the exchange seems favorable. Sadly, this is all too common in our most intimate relationships, where we love another not simply for their being, but for those things that they provide that fulfill parts of ourselves never weaned from our parents' uncompleted efforts.

Put simply, in Fromm's framework, Western society inhibits us from ever fully maturing, with respect to love of self and others and the world around us. Love in the natural human, he says, *is an attitude, an orientation of character which determines the relatedness of a person to the world as a whole, not toward one 'object' of love. If a person loves only one other person and is indifferent to the rest of his fellow men, his love is not love but a symbiotic attachment, or an enlarged egotism.*

Is this kind of love even possible anymore?

The principle underlying capitalistic society and the principle of love are incompatible, Fromm concludes – and after examining his argument in detail, it's hard to refute. But he goes on: *People capable of love, under our present system, are necessarily the exceptions... those who are seriously concerned with love as the only rational answer to the problem of human existence must, then, arrive at the conclusion that important and radical changes in our social structure are necessary, if love is to become a social and not a highly individualistic, marginal phenomenon.*

Can we get there from here? Do we even want to anymore?

Zero-Sum Thinking

The core of inequality - the core of warfare, the core of racism, the core of religion - is the idea that for some to win, others must lose.

This is a major factor in the Authoritarian dynamic: the Leader rallies Followers by pointing out Others, and labeling the Others a Threat –*They* will take your food! *They* will take your jobs! *They* are the wrong that must be corrected!

Call it Zero-Sum Thinking.

Zero-Sum Thinking: the pool of resources is limited, so in order for some to have more, others must have less.

So we must invent some criteria by which those who take more can justify others getting less.

It seems awkward to reduce such an emotionally-charged phenomenon to mathematics, but here it is: this dynamic is completely pointless when the pool of resources *isn't* limited.

And this gives us a major piece of the human puzzle: inequality, which gave rise to social classes, hierarchies, racism, and eventually Authoritarianism and warfare, didn't (couldn't) exist until resources were made finite.

Welcome to the Upper Paleolithic, where resources abound, despite the Ice Age.

We find not a single instance of evidence of organized conflict anywhere in our excavation of the ancient African past for two very good reasons: 1) it was an unacceptable risk, and 2) it was utterly unnecessary.

Human tribes were migratory for millions of years, and with good reason - constantly moving from one territory to another meant a constant refreshing of resources (the entire point of migration). There was always plenty of food in all directions, when one territory had been well-picked over. When two tribes overlapped, the idea of conflict would have been unthinkable: risk our young hunters dying? Why? There's food in the next valley, and we survive because of our numbers! Risking death to hold a territory we must leave soon anyway would be insane...

Excess population in any one territory, then, did nothing more than prime the migratory pump: it didn't hurt human tribes, it helped. Once a territory was vacated, Nature took over and replenished the food supply, via routine growth. All of life, unfettered by human industry, renews.

Why? Because resources weren't limited. So there was never any motivation to think in zero-sum terms.

Where, then, did zero-sum thinking in human social order originate? It started when resources *were* limited.

When we learned to plant food and pen it up for later slaughter, we committed to fixed blocks of land. And any fixed block is resource-limited. *Now* we have reason to fight! *Now* we have reason to risk death. After a few generations, our skill at gathering energy from the land, wherever we may be, atrophies - and zero-sum thinking takes hold. If too many people occupy some block of land, then some having more means others having less.

And so it goes, for more than 10,000 years. Most, if not all, of human misery derives from this unfortunate shift.

Must we return to the nomadic existence of small tribes in order to recover our species virtue? No. We have the resources, technological and economic, to craft a planet that can provide for all - where there is no more zero-sum, where no one must be consigned to having less. What we lack is the social and political will to undertake this crafting. And why is that? There is no good intellectual reason, only the angry and defensive emotions that have accumulated over 100 centuries.

We should think long and hard about that...

"As man advances in civilization, and small tribes
are united into larger communities, the simplest
reason would tell each individual that he ought to
extend his social instincts and sympathies to all
the members of the same nation, though
personally unknown to him. This point being once
reached, there is only an artificial barrier to
prevent his sympathies extending to the men of all
nations and races."

~Charles Darwin

The Grown-Up in the Room

Be the grown-up in the room.

The political and social animosity is flowing like river water over a damn, chasing in every direction through every opening. It has to stop.

There are behaviors and acts that should be shouted down and, in some cases, ridiculed. There are dangerous ideas in the air that should be loudly opposed.

But the personal attacks, the petulance, the Our Side v. Their Side - that doesn't help, it only adds to the flooding.

Defending Our Thoughts

As citizens of a Western nation, we are already accustomed to a certain level of freedom in thought - though this is by no means a universal condition, nor even a very old one. It has long been the way of human society that any regional or national grouping of human beings be required to conform, in thought and action, to the biases of its ruling class. Western civilization has moved, for a handful of centuries, at least, in another direction. And we are heirs to the benefits of that motion.

On the face of it, our new digital society pushes this freedom even further; we are at liberty to express all manner of thought, no matter how outlandish, no matter how ill-informed, no matter how obscene, and no stormtroopers will gather in our doorway. But there's a step between *Think as Your Leaders Tell You To* and *I Can Say Anydamnthing I Please* that we are missing, and it may be the most important step in human discourse.
Free as we are to think and say what we please, we are no longer required to explain or defend our thoughts and words.

When we crawled out from under the English boot and began to express our notions of religious freedom, we were not shy about our opinions of the king and his church. When we decided we wanted to be a nation unto ourselves, governing ourselves, we were not shy (or lacking eloquence) in articulating our position.

And when we went to war with one another, brother rising up against brother, we were forced to defend our awkward stands.

But that was then. Today, via the supplementary voices with which technology has imbued us, it is all too easy to jump on board a train of opinion and enjoy the music of our own minds, echoing from every direction. We are rolling further and further from the station, from the noise and bustle of many minds, from the need to justify our point of view, soothed by the soft caress of consensus.

And our minds grow complacent. And in that complacence is a growth medium for error, and in the end, the atrophies that the changing world around us will inevitably bring.

Why do I believe what I believe? *Why* does this idea seem right to me? *How* did I arrive at this position? These questions insist that we think and feel and speak and act in good faith and for good reasons - but we have created a social marketplace where we never need ask them again. The emotional safety of church/political party/website/twitterfeed has obscured the rational gymnastics that spurred our foreparents to board ships, across perilous seas to very distant shores; it silences the timeless words that justified the brutally difficult work of creating a nation where self-government was even possible, and the crafting of cradles for new, world-changing ideas that required both pen and musket for survival.

In short, the safety of like-mindedness is no safety at all; it is no philosophical haven, it is an emotional sauna; an intellectual graveyard, not a righteous pantheon.

Our beliefs and convictions and the thoughts and feelings that enable them cannot survive in the real world, apart from the fawning gluttonies of the accommodating, without frequent and rigorous scrutiny from within, in the privacy of our own deliberations, and even more frequent presentation to those who stand elsewhere. It is the walk in the evening air, the shouldering of a burden down a long path that strengthens the body and sharpens the senses; and it is the defense of our ideas and articulation of our point of view, the presentation of the Why and How over and above the What, that bolsters our cognition and vindicates our emotions.

And that's before we even get to listening...

Farewell to Sunday School

Prediction: Authoritarian religions in the West have blown it, and their mistake is unrecoverable - they have triggered an attrition cycle from which they cannot recover.

I call this a prediction, but I'm not yet ready to really put it forth as such - more study is needed, so let's just call this a tentative hypothesis. Others have worked on this with me a bit, we'll see what he thinks about pushing forward with it.

Per Ron Sider, Christian sociologist and author of *The Scandal of the Evangelical Conscience* (and per observations and stats gathered previously by others), the Fundamentalist institution of Sunday School has been steadily dying off for more than 20 years.

Since the mid-Nineties, churches have invested less and less in that Sunday morning exercise of indoctrinating the young, filling them with Bible stories and lessons from the age they could first speak. Countless generations have grown up with this sort of religious instruction (myself included), the result of which is an individual whose entire worldview is framed according to Fundamentalist assumptions.

This, combined with the power of the social isolation practiced within Evangelical communities, has a staggeringly powerful effect on the growing mind. Our individual rules for living emerge from our beliefs about the world and others, and those beliefs come in two flavors: experiential belief and social belief. The first means "I believe this because of what I've seen and heard"; the second means "I believe this because I have learned it from my social group." Sunday School, in concert with social isolation, combines the two into one.

When the opportunity for alternative experience + social learning from other groups occurs, religious belief (and Authoritarian belief in particular) diminishes (see Altemeyer). This is why we have Christian home-schooling, Christian high schools and Christian colleges - to limit the exposure of Christian young people to people and ideas outside the fold. Sunday School is at the root of all of these, a powerful inoculation occurring not long after birth, with regular boosters.

But the level of isolation required to maintain this social frame is increasingly difficult to sustain in the modern world. The Internet, social media, mobile computing and the very nature of social interaction among the young make it so. The incoming generation - the Millennials - are the first to have travelled from childhood to adulthood with these tools in hand and these communication patterns ingrained from Day One, and we can see with only a casual glance that they, as a result, see the world and other people differently than their predecessors.

Sunday School has faded because of the Evangelical church's preoccupation with wealth and influence, and the growing reality that it became a cost center, rather than a revenue generator. Put another way, it has become so hard to hold the attention of young people that more and more money had to be spent entertaining them, to keep them coming back, and that money was better invested in the outer commons coffee bar.

That was a fatal mistake.

When Sunday School goes away, both the installation and maintenance of the social frame that sustains the Fundamentalist worldview likewise vanish. Sunday School was the ace-in-the-hole of Authoritarian religion: it isn't the preacher's sermon or the group chants or the latest Evangelical best-seller that keep the adult Authoritarian follower in the pew (and notice, by the way, how all those things have had to change over the past 20 years in order to remain in place) - it's the imperviousness of that adult to ideas and perceptions from without. And that imperviousness, for the overwhelming majority, was implanted in childhood.

Put simply, without Sunday School, Evangelical religions have no means of sustaining their populations. The generation that should have come through Sunday School, and the young now forming the next, are too skeptical, too experiential, too deeply connected to ever take Bible stories - let alone the dire pronouncements and broad condemnations of their elders - even a little bit seriously. They are lost to the church, and will be unrecoverable, even when they themselves become parents.

What is left? Only one sub-population: Authoritarian followers who are faithful to the church only because it is Authoritarian - those adults who would go find another church if theirs became even a little bit socially progressive. And their children - those who share their predisposition, anyway - will remain, only because Dad Says So.

But that sub-population can't sustain a megachurch. And the megachurch now defines modern Evangelicalism.

Worse yet for Evangelical America, the Millennials not only have bullshit detectors too keen to ever give them a pass - they also have superior ethics, and through the most egregious means: their moral formation has happened outside of an in-group. The Millennials, because of their enhanced connectedness and early exposure to so much of the world, have formed a moral frame more through observation than inheritance - and maybe be the first generation in civilized history to have done so.

Put it all together and it's a pretty bleak picture for Fundamentalism. When the institution's young are leaving in droves, and its existence now hinges on its ability to attract new ones, it's pretty harsh to claim to be the place for people who want to do what's right, and the generation that really wants to be in that place answers, 'So do we, but that certainly isn't you...'

The Millennials Shall Inherit the Earth

Premise: Millennials (people born between the early 80s and early 2000s) are not just a new generation; they are a generation different-in-kind. Their attitudes about politics, government, religion, and Western society are taking a different direction than those of previous generations. They do not simply distrust the world of their parents; they are disinterested in it; they are, to put it mildly, unimpressed.

This is to say that they see little merit in the institutions that surround them - and I suspect there will be considerable creative destruction when they come to power, and not of the kind we've seen perpetually attempted by the Conservative Right over the past generation.

Why do I think this? I see so many differences between the social and economic universe of my children and myself that I can scarcely list them all:

- Their level of engagement with the world began much sooner and ran much deeper than mine. They are the first generation to have an Internet available to them even before they reached the age of socialization. Their information channels - millions of websites, hundreds of TV sources - are virtually limitless, and they have had it all at their fingertips since before they could read. I had three TV channels and *Time* magazine.

- Their personal communications are likewise far more complex. Millennials have been immersed in digital interpersonal communication as long as they have been communicating with others; they know no other life. They have email; they have text; they have social media; they have web forums; they carry phones with them wherever they go, and the phones facilitate all the other channels. I had a telephone on a wall, stationery and stamps in a desk drawer, and passed notes in the back of the classroom.

- The social groups they engage in are available on demand. A Millennial has grown up so connected to others, and their social group-of-choice in particular, that they need never disengage unless they choose to. Group chats in text, social media groups, carefully-crafted friends lists - all of these serve to provide immediate social gratification. It's all available to me, too, but only in this most recent 20% of my life: this level of engagement was not only impossible but undreamed-of when I was growing up, and only got together with my inner circles in person, and then only when it was logistically convenient for all.

What does all of this add up to?

First, it underscores that the human condition up to this point in history has been relative social isolation. From the dawn of cities and ethnic groups to my own generation, children were integrated into the family's home, coming and going mostly together, and then to institutions of the parents' choosing. The social universe did not expand for a child until well into adolescence, and then, usually, only into opportunity provided by the family social circle.

This is no longer the case. The Millennials are the first generation to enjoy on-demand bridges into other social domains in early adolescence and often before. Not only are they unconstrained by their parents' social selection, they are able to make individual choices about who to include/exclude in the social collectives they construct.

Second, channels of information about the world have steadily increased as technology has proliferated over the past century - from newspapers and word-of-mouth only to print-plus-radio-and-TV and public libraries, to the Cambrian explosion of channels available now, in the digital era. I thought I had it good, compared to my parents; I thought I was blessed to have so little distance between me and news of the world. The instant access to ALL knowledge available to the Millennial makes me look like a Cro-Magnon roaming around looking for cave paintings. Again, I have access to everything the Millennials have today - but they've had it all their lives, while my generation is still struggling to adapt.

Finally, all of this digital goodness has resulting infar greater levels of for-better-or-worse transparency into the institutions that I grew up with. The workings of government, the behaviors of the religious, the nuts and bolts of the economy, the news-behind-the-news - all of these things were obscure, in varying degrees, in my youth; if I wanted the inside scoop, I had to wait for *Sixty Minutes*, and hope that whichever journalist was presenting the story asked the probing questions that were on my mind.

Not so, today: the world my parents' parents built, that my parents' generation corrupted and that my generation bungled, is now bare-ass naked in the glaring light of 24/7 infotainment and citizen journalism. A young person growing up immersed in that noise can scarcely emerge with a single smidgen of the passive trust and bedtime-story confidence that I enjoyed, believing the world would be fine tomorrow morning.

So fast was all of this new technology upon us that no one fully understood the psychosocial impact of this flood of information on pre-adolescent minds - so no one could anticipate it would result in a new generation wired, not only to see the world differently, but to understand it in completely new ways. This leads us to wonder, not only what kind of world the Millennials will build, but what kind of world they will even want.

What happens next isn't altogether clear. The Millennials don't trust the world they are inheriting, and they don't fully appreciate the superpowers they are absorbing from its light and heat. Moreover, in their indifference to the workings of their parents' world, they are not picking up the tools needed to renovate it. They have no desire to perpetuate its institutions, but present no real idea what to replace them with.

I'm glad they're going to take the reins, and I'm encouraged that they'll be more skeptical than my generation has been - and more on their guard, and better at bullshit detection. But I wish my kids would ask me a question or two, every now and then, about how we got here and why, and where those tools are actually stored - in case they ever take a mind to start using them...

Fear, Anger, Hatred

When we're afraid, we're not paying attention - to anything other than what's making us afraid.

When we're angry, we're not thinking - not leaving enough space in our heads for pursing a solution for whatever it is that is upsetting us.
When we hate, we shut out both attention and thought - no path back or around whatever is stirring darkness within us.

Fear, anger and hatred are all natural emotions - and they are almost always misapplied, as so many of our emotions are in this artificial world of ours. The neutral truth is that there are very, very few things we should fear, very few things that should make us angry, and almost no good reasons for hatred.

More so because all three of these emotions are enemies of clear thought and good judgment. When our brains are preoccupied with these toxic feelings, we aren't solving the problem, we aren't even seeing it clearly - and our attention and our judgment go to hell.

But we have another place in our minds where we *do* solve problems, we *do* see clearly, we *do* locate our good judgment. Choosing to be there, rather than in our uglier emotions, is a win-win - our issues don't go unsolved, and our thoughts are not wasted.

Darwin's Simplest Reason

"As man advances in civilization, and small tribes are united into larger communities, the simplest reason would tell each individual that he ought to extend his social instincts and sympathies to all the members of the same nation, though personally unknown to him. This point being once reached, there is only an artificial barrier to prevent his sympathies extending to the men of all nations and races."

~Charles Darwin

Darwin is right. Is there one among us (and I mean in this group, not the entire human race) who doesn't realize, intellectually, that all human beings are of a kind, and that those we don't know are inherently worthy of the same basic respect we dispense to those we do?

Why, then, the systematic devaluation of entire ethnicities? Why the daily demeaning of those who disagree with us about matters utterly abstract (and even imaginary)? Why the cultivation of contempt as entertainment, and why the serves-them-right celebration when those outside our circle stumble?

We've seen that Dunbar's Number gives us a starting point: our cortical mass, in that region where social processing occurs, can accommodate a certain number of intimate relationships and no more, a constraint suffered by every living human being; relationships are memory- and processing-intensive, consuming vast amounts of brainpower, and there simply isn't enough tissue in our brains to handle more than a small churchful of people up there. But that doesn't explain it all.

On the surface of Dunbar, we lower the value of non-intimates for lack of brainpower to know them, if our social cortex is already full, because out-of-memory; but, of course, we have reasoning powers beyond our social capacity for intimacy. We don't need to have brains large enough to intimately know everyone we meet in order to vindicate Darwin's thesis. It should not be too great a leap to think as Darwin suggests - as he puts it, "the simplest reason" should get us there.

But several factors work against that.

First, we are surrounded by leaders (and their followers) who leverage our intimacy limits in order to lower the value of those human beings they find convenient (or profitable) to disenfranchise. We experience a degree of cognitive relief when the emotional requirements of Darwin's admonition are set aside: it's easier to dismiss strangers than to extend humanity to them. And it's *much* easier to shun an entire people than to go through the exhaustive steps of reconciling their strange ways, thoughts and practices with our own. Rooting out are common humanity, in such a diverse world, takes substantial effort that is easier avoided, and those who would control us trade on that.

Second, we have concocted a world that works against the natural empathy of the human mind. Evolution has predisposed us for deep cooperation, for living intimately in close tribes, for sharing food and warmth and thought and feeling with others of our kind, for living and dying as one. No other creature under the firmaments can match the empathy of a human being. But our cultivated inequality, our hierarchical parsing of who is and who isn't, our dedication to lifting some and lowering others is a vast damper on those natural inclinations. We live, day by day, in an empathy-crushing envelope of human insensitivity and passive derision, driven not by our innate hunger for the company of our own kind but by the fleeting, sugary slurp of politic flatteries within our tribal circles. It is no wonder our natural affection for our own kind wanes.

Finally, there is our misdirected love of self - the endless thump of cultural drums, beating into us the idea that our value as human beings is that which makes us stand out, not that which we hold in common. We are not "special" because we are human beings to begin with; we are "special" because something about us is unique, or so we tell ourselves. Society's script informs us that to be "ordinary" is to be less than valuable, that we rise and fall in the eyes of those around us according to our publicly-paraded individuality.

But "difference," and even uniqueness, is built into our genes; we can't help but host some set of traits that makes our selfie stand apart. This is where we put our effort and attention, but an awkward truth intrudes: if we could simply take the step of realizing that humanity itself is the core of what makes us special, then those unique features that inhabit us all would jump out in high relief, to self and others. We focus on flower, not fruit, and in so doing skip over the real treasures of being human.

So important is the issue of our selective disconnection that it is quickly becoming a make-or-break moment for our species. We are fast approaching our tipping point on this home planet of ours, doubling our numbers in less than a single human lifetime; our tensions are rising, our fear and anger increasing. Most issues before the human congress aren't binary, but this one is increasingly so: either we will relocate Darwin's simplest reason, and realize that in the end we still stand or fall together - or we won't, and it will be everyone for themselves, a condition we are not built to survive.

A Handy Guide to Surviving a Meeting at Another Company

There you sit, surrounded by people you don't know, discussing matters of heavy gravity, with much at stake. You don't know where you stand with them; you don't know where they stand with each other; and you don't know how you'll navigate the uncertain terrain of your business negotiations while simultaneously trying to puzzle out How Things Work Here.

Well, here's your Uncle Scott to guide you through this perplexing morass! First, wait for someone to say something really, really dumb.

Then look at everyone *except* the person who said it. Their responses to the dumb thing will tell you who they are.

- The people who smile enthusiastically are other dumb people;

- The person who smiles and nods is the stakeholder who knows it's dumb, but has a lot riding on it;

- The person who smiles and frowns wishes he'd said the dumb thing first;

- The people who find something in the room to stare at have all heard the dumb thing before, wish it hadn't been said, and do not want to be called on next;

- The people who stare right at you also realize it's dumb, and are concerned about your response;

- The people who pause and then frown are the smartest people in the room - they are pondering the consequences of the dumb thing being said, but are not staring at you because they have already figured you out and are less concerned with your response than that of their peers.

Got it? Now you know the lay of the land. The question is, what next?

If they all turn and look at you after a minute, it's definitely on you to respond. Here are some safe go-to standards:

"That's interesting..." - an ambiguous, safe return, like a straight-line Pong volley, putting it back on the room;

"Could you elaborate?" - taking the upper hand; feed the dumb person some rope, to improve your position;

"I'm not sure I fully understand..." - this likewise puts it back on the room, but confirms to the smart people in the room (as well as the stakeholder) that you did not just fall off the turnip truck, and are as aware of the dumbness as they are, and someone had better start tap-dancing.

But the best response of all gets you out of there just long enough to end the awkward moment, allow them to regroup, and present themselves again - and now you truly *do* have the upper hand, because now you know the lay of the land:

"Where did you say the restroom was?"

"The big difference when [a child today] grows up - in fact you won't have to wait for the year 2001 - is that he will have in his own house ... a console through which he can talk to his friendly local computer and get all the information he needs for his everyday life, like his bank statements, theatre reservations - all the information you need in the course of living in a complex modern society. This will be in a compact form in his own house. You"ll have a television screen…and a keyboard and he'll talk to the computer and get information from it. And he'll take it as much for granted as we take the telephone."

~Arthur C. Clarke, 1974

The Right Answer

The solution is not for Democrats to "win". The solution is not for the GOP to "lose".

The solution is for all of us to stop thinking in terms of party, and to begin reaching beyond our immediate circles and learning to listen to and talk to those who don't think as we do.

When *any* political party "wins" in taking power and dominating policy, *everyone* loses. Any one like-minded consortium of policymakers can, by definition, only deliver solutions that cater to their own cognitive style. Leadership and policy-making that accommodates the citizenry at large can only emerge from a cognitively diverse body of policymakers.

When we huddle together with those who see things as we do, we weaken ourselves cognitively, truncating our capacity to reason out even those views most firmly embraced; our ability to honestly and fairly evaluate other arguments gradually atrophies, leaving only the tired echoes of dogma and the received wisdom of our private hierarchies. And our personal cognitive infirmities are only amplified, when the group acts as a whole; our group's thoughts and assumptions, weak to begin with, ceased to be reasoned positions at all, and become identity markers, and little more.

We can be strong again. We can get back to the system our Founding Fathers created, a system that eschewed parties altogether. Finding that place requires that we let go of the idea that "my party's ideas are best for the population overall," and realize that that statement can never be true, and rediscover real discourse, real debate, and how it feels to achieve conviction by walking the hard path of real dialog.

"Let us not seek the Republican answer or the Democratic answer, but the right answer. Let us not seek to fix the blame for the past. Let us accept our own responsibility for the future."

~John F. Kennedy

The Real World in Our Heads

Our brains are only so big. They only hold so much information. They can only accommodate a certain number of relationships with other people. In short, no one human brain can contain the entirety of what the world throws at us.

Our brains can absorb some facts about the world around us, some memories of what's happened to us, good outcomes versus bad, and a limited ability to look ahead and figure out what might happen next. We're limited in all of these by what our brains can handle.

This is true of all creatures, and is true in more-or-less equal measure for all human beings. This is a firm physical limitation, based on the volume of our skulls and the number of connections possible inside our skulls. There's no way around these numbers.

The world we perceive, then, isn't the actual real world - it's a limited representation of that world, a model, an incomplete picture that we assemble out of our experience and the knowledge we accumulate over time. There are gaps. There are mistakes. And the same is true (to an even greater degree) for all the other creatures who inhabit the globe.

We have an advantage, however, that other creatures don't: we have each other. What does exist inside our limited skulls is pretty marvelous, more powerful than the best the rest of life on earth can muster, and it includes a big chunk of brain that's set aside for social connection, social knowledge, social reasoning. We have each other, and that means that our brains can be networked - we can tap into the knowledge and experience of others, and boost our ability to look ahead and figure out what happens next.

Put another way - because we are such deeply social creatures, sharing our knowledge and learning from one another's experience, we are capable of building world models not just individually but together.

That seems like a good thing, doesn't it? At our deepest core, the world model in our head is ultimately personal, based on our own wanderings and conclusions about them. But rather than syncing that model to the actual world, we are able to sync it to the greater model that we and the people around us have created between us - a model that fills in the gaps in our own, and corrects our mistakes.

Unless...

...unless the world model we build together doesn't reflect the actual real world.

Realizing that a "group model" of the world is going to contain information and experience gathered by other minds, we have to survey who, exactly, is contributing to that model. What do we find?

For the past 100 centuries, those group models have been assembled by large numbers of people with the same or similar thoughts, the same or similar experiences, the same or similar manner of interpretation. In short: the group models of the world created by people in cognitive clusters isn't going to be much of an improvement over an individual world model in a single mind. It will present the illusion of completeness, it will seem to fill in gaps, and it will appear to correct mistakes - but more likely it will amplify mistakes, fill gaps with conjecture rather than knowledge, and dismiss experience from without.

And that's what we see, when we examine the views of reality presented by congregations of the like-minded: a systematic distancing, and sometimes outright denial, of reality; a constant repetition of mistakes that overwhelms the basic learning mechanism in the brain of the individual; and a contrived facade that may be emotionally satisfying, but which often obscures what is real to a degree that actually cultivates danger to both the individual and the group that embraces it.

It's tempting to roll back that extra layer of world-modeling, to simply rely on our innate personal construct. But that one is physically limited to an unacceptable degree, and there's no way around that. We are left with solitary recourse: cultivate a collective world-model, but built that model with the knowledge and experience of minds unlike our own; build that model with knowledge and experience that really will fill in the gaps and correct the mistakes.

That, of course, is far more work - and much harder work - than simply
believing that our own view of the world is right because the people who
agree with us say it is. On the other side of that hard work, however, is a
prize no other beings in all the world can claim: the power to walk thru the
world with perception and understanding unmatched by any other creature
(or less aware people), not simply experiencing reality, but commanding it.

"We exist in a bizarre combination of Stone Age emotions, medieval beliefs, and god-like technology."

~E.O. Wilson

No Win

If Trump is unseated, the Left hasn't "won."

If the GOP goes down in flames in the Midterms, the Democrats haven't "won."

If conservative politicians fade away for the next generation, the progressives haven't "won."

There could be no worse reaction to the Right's current self-immolation than for its opponents to embrace some sense of "victory." There isn't anything more destructive, not only to US politics but to the social fabric of the West than our insane devotion to echo chamber community.

A Left "victory" over the Right is no more a victory than the Right's "victory" in 2016; when *any* partisan force "wins," we all lose.

A "win" would be all of those not in the GOP bubble - mainstream Dems, Bernie fans, libertarians, greens, moderate Republicans - everyone not on the Trump Train or the Ryan-McConnell obstruction machine banding together and agreeing that disagreeing is not only *not* a bad thing, it's a healthy thing - and not just a healthy thing, but exactly what the nation needs, a return to real discourse, real listening, real negotiation, real mutual understanding. A "win" is a consortium of adults who let go of their partisan fetishes and return to the true national conversation.

We are the core of that consortium. We are the adults who have to set the example. We have to find humility now, in this moment when it is so easy to feel self-righteous and justified.

This is the moment to admit that we are just as guilty of pouring our time, money and emotions into a rigged slot machine for the cheap thrill of watching things spin. Now is the time to confess that our answers aren't good just because theirs are terrible.

There's one "win," and only one: united we stand, divided we fall. Don't add to the divide - not today, not tomorrow, not at all.

The Money Metaphor

We think in metaphor. This is the conclusion of the leading cognitive scientists of our day, including Douglas Hofstadter, whose conclusion that "*This* is like *That*" forms the core of our cognitive facility rests at the center of his theory of cognition. George Lakoff, author of *Metaphors We Live By*, ably demonstrates that how we conceive both the physical and social universe depends almost entirely upon the metaphors we absorb as we learn and mature.

It is both a blessing and a curse that we have increased the complexity of the world in which we all must live, and so in turn we've increased the consequences of the metaphors we adopt in order to more accurately perceive and understand it.

Few are the domains of thought where our core metaphor has greater impact than our understanding of economics. To a large degree, the range of understanding of economics evident in our discourse sees largely ideological - and it is, somewhat - but it takes only a few moments of chatting with someone about the economy to see that, ideology aside, some people cling fiercely to whatever metaphor makes the flow of money clear to them.

"Mary. mother of God, am I *sick* of that insane analogy!" screams Slone Sabbith (Olivia Munn) in an episode of *The Newsroom*: "Balancing your checkbook is to balancing the budget as driving to the supermarket is to landing on the moon!!!" And she's right.

Here is a useful metaphorical spectrum, showing how far you can go just with "money is water":

Money is Like Rainfall: It comes and goes, and we catch what we can, and the supply at any given moment is limited.

Money is Like a River: It's a never-ending stream, as value is always being created at the source, and as it flows we can take some out and put some back in and alter the flow, redirecting it here and there.

Money is Like Aquifers: It permeates society, accumulating in places, flowing in others, seeping in others, endlessly cyclic.

Money is Like Oceans: It feeds the sky, it sends itself in all directions, it carries energy, it deposits itself in lakes and ponds, it accepts the returns of rivers, it is eternally moving.

Notice that each of these metaphors has its own strengths and limitations. And notice, next time you have a conversation about economics with someone who sees it differently, that they will have their own innate perceptions of the strengths and limitations of money transfer - and that it will be hard to move them off those perceptions.

We can go much farther in our understanding of money if we choose the right metaphor, as Lakoff demonstrates. Here's my best pitch:

Money is Energy.

When I choose this metaphor, I don't have the optional range of perceptions that "water" bestows - energy is necessarily a big pool of dynamics that force me to think through any statement I make about economics. Money is *literally* a stand-in for energy: it originated as markers for edible commodities, a stand-in for the trading of food, and even in the contemporary marketplace, all monetary exchanges eventually reduce to energy trades.

If "Money is Energy," then money *never* dead-ends; it cycles infinitely.

It endlessly changes form; 'value', cycling thru its ecosphere, means something different in each form.

If it sits in one place, it becomes subject to entropy, and dissipates (inflation).

It can be channeled to perform Work, with the efficiency of that rechanneling necessarily varying.

The greater the quantity, the greater the potential for destruction.

Each agent consuming it has an optimal carrying capacity; too little, and death results; too much, and death results.

Now we're talking economics...

"I am made from the dust of the stars, and the ocean flows in my veins..."

~Neil Peart, Rush

AI on the Trail

On this beautiful Sunday, I'm hiking in the park with Starbuck, and after a 10-minute silence, she suddenly pops up with, "Daddy? When, how, and why will sentient artificial intelligence threaten humanity?"

Wow. My heart did a somersault, I was so happy to get that question! I mentioned that this was actually a current topic among my colleagues, and that even the most expert opinions varied. We are not nearly as close to machine sentience as exposure to Siri and Alexa might lead one to assume, I explained, and the truth is that we are not at all sure of our footing in even correctly defining the problem, let alone to proceeding to design.

First, we discussed "sentience" - its definition is complex, but let's settle for "self-awareness." There is no common state exemplifying it, I told her: human beings are self-aware in ways other primates are not; primates are self-aware in ways dogs and elephants and dolphins are not; and so on, down the line. So, when we talk about artificial "sentience," are we talking human-like, or otherwise?

We decided to go with "human-like sentience = able to understand and share our values."

That led us to "values = rules by which we implement our moral judgments," and this led us into trouble. A Google car can be programmed to handle the high-traffic equivalent of the Trolley Problem, but does that represent values? No, moral judgments and behaviors are rule-based events, which *follow* from values - they are not actual values themselves.

HAL-9000, I told her, possessed human-like social behavior which caused his creator and colleagues to assume human-like thought - yet HAL did not have our values. He murdered the crew of *Discovery*, the darkest violation of human morality.

How, Starbuck wanted to know, could a sentient AI absorb human values? I suggested that it couldn't be via programming, since programming amounts to rules, and we had already seen that rules follow values, but are not values themselves. My answer: a sentient AI would need to learn values by sharing human experience.

Like Data, on *ST:TNG*. Data shares human values, despite being an android (and superior to humans in many ways) - and does so because he learned them, by living among them.

But, she wanted to know, what about Data's 'brother' Lore, also an android? And an identical one?

That only underscores the point, I answered: Lore is immoral, by human standards, despite being physically identical to Data. The only difference between them is their experiences among humans; Lore's were less than positive, leading to a different value system.

And this led her to ask, "How do emotions figure in sentient AI?" My answer was, For any sentience that could have any hope of being human-like, emotions are essential - our brains are 'layered,' an ancient brain wrapped in a newer one, wrapped in a newer one, leading to our current level of sophistication. We still retain every layer, and the most ancient is our core emotions - the limbic system - which was our original decision-making system, our basic intelligence. Even HAL-9000 had this one: the instinct to fight to survive.

But, she wondered, "Wasn't Skynet emotional? Didn't it want to wipe out humanity out of malevolence?"

"That's a tough one," I replied. "Even within the canon, interpretations differ. The most useful one for our purposes is that Skynet was created as an integrated platform for the global management of humanity, and upon achieving self-awareness, Skynet concluded that the greatest threat to the management of humanity was humanity - and that the elimination of that obstacle left a worthwhile, persistent result... Skynet."

"Yet Data wasn't emotional," she pointed out, "and wanted emotions more than anything."

"To be a real boy," I nodded. And then she made the leap, "Like Andrew Martin in *The Bicentennial Man*." My heart swelled to bursting. I raised her right!

I told her that Gene Roddenberry had maintained a 25-year friendship with Isaac Asimov, who created Andrew Martin (played by Robin Williams in the 1998 movie version), an android serving a human family who achieve self-awareness, loves the family, and wishes to earn the right to be called 'human' by humanity. Roddenberry could not have been unaware of the Hugo-winning story of Andrew, and was certainly inspired in the creation of Data by it (though I strongly suspect David Gerrold had more than a little to do with Data's development as a character). In the real world, I don't believe that Data or Andrew Martin could achieve the value systems they do, shared experience with humans or not, without emotions - without a 'limbic chip' - but the characters do much to stimulate our thinking about the problem.

I offered her the conclusion that 1) sentient, "self-aware" AI is not only possible but probably not far off, but it will not be human-like sentience; 2) it will be achieved through the agency of many AIs interacting and learning from each other, adapting to the outcomes that follow from their interaction, and 3) if this proves threatening or fatal to humanity, it will be accidental, not malicious.

And if such an intelligence ever presents itself, I will hasten to arrange an introduction to Starbuck...

Quality of Contemplation

We need not mock all ideas that are wrong, let alone fear them. Our task is to explore the thinking that went into them.

Here are two examples. Elaine Morgan wrote a number of provocative books that explore the possibilities of the human past. One was an advancing of the Aquatic Ape theory, a suggestion that human evolution was critically dependent upon a relationship with the ocean - an idea that the scientific community ultimately rejected. We can set aside Aquatic Ape theory while still admiring the elegance of Morgan's reasoning.

The same is true of Julian Jaynes, who advanced the idea of the bicameral mind, a possible explanation for human self-awareness - that the two halves of the brain once "talked" to each other, initiating a sophisticated loop of cognitive self-attention that eventually became our consciousness. This, too, is an idea that science has set aside - but Jaynes' argument is admirably clear and clever.

The point is simple: it's not always about being "right", which no idea can ever completely be, anyway; it's about the quality of contemplation, and learning to express ideas in clear, compelling ways. We have way too much focus on being "right" - and not nearly enough focus on quality of contemplation...

"Once we have computer outlets in every home, each of them hooked up to enormous libraries, where you can ask any question and be given answers, you can look up something you're interested in knowing, however silly it might seem to someone else."

~Isaac Asimov

Affirmation Addiction

We are addicted to agreement.

We strongly gravitate to those who agree with us. We seek out those who say we are right. There is no greater pleasure for the young child than the praise of the parent or the teacher when the right answer is given, and a disorienting feeling of unease when we are told we are wrong. We subdue the latter over time, as we mature, and are free to let the former run rampant.

And run rampant it does: our glee at being told we are right is up there with wine, sex and ice cream on our scale of sought-after pleasures.

Being told we are right is affirmation. It is validation that we are accepted, listened to, a meaningful presence in the room. It doesn't matter if the affirmation is contrived, gratuitous, or even a calculated manipulation: our emotional response is built in, immediate, irrepressible, and for better or worse, it's an important reinforcement of who we are.

To be sure, there are exceptions: there are those among us who think what they think and feel what they feel and don't give a rat's ass what anyone else thinks – but they are the isolated cranks among us, off in a corner snubbing the rest of us, and they are the exception that proves the rule. The rest of us want to hear, *need* to hear that we are right, that our ideas and emotions and responses to the world are considered valid by others.

This impulse, so ingrained and passive that we seldom if ever give it conscious thought, is a defining feature of our social behavior. Our hunger for that feeling of 'rightness' in our thought and behavior is nestled into the core of our feelings about who we are and what we believe and how we should act – and all of that is, in turn, a reflection of the actual machinery of the social brain. We are, *by nature's design*, beings who need to feel an alignment of our thoughts and feelings with those of others.
So, isn't this a good thing?

Not an easy question. It was a good thing tens of thousands of years ago, when groups of humans were faced with a group decision and a group reaction was required; to bring new information into that decision was certainly a good thing, and the 'rightness' of the information and the subsequent decision had a direct impact on the group, for better or worse. Today, however, that 'rightness' meter in our brains is not so deeply connected with the actual world. It is perfectly possible - in fact, commonplace – to get that *ping* of 'rightness' over information that is completely wrong.

Moreover – and far, far worse! - the *ping* can basically become a reward for being wrong.

Put simply, *feeling* right can become far more important than actually *being* right. Our desire for the feeling of affirmation can, and often does, override our allegiance to what is real.

This is a feature of the social human that has been noted (and relentlessly exploited) for millennia: the social dominator understands, through observation, that the people surrounding him will, once they receive affirmation, pursue that affirmation unquestioningly. It then becomes simple to merely call out those 'rightness' prompts, and let them *ding* themselves into lock-step obedience.

It's easy to laugh at this, even to mock it - but the brutal truth is that we all are subject to this impulse, to one degree or another. Even the disciples of science, who spend a lifetime suppressing the *ping* in favor of reality, require years and years of training to even begin to succeed at it – and even then, often unravel in their later years, doggedly clinging to this idea or that, as new information abandons them to irrelevance.

The result isn't just unfortunate – it's potentially catastrophic. When we set aside what's real in favor of the intellectual pat-on-the-head from those as ignorant (or more) as we, there is a self-defeating/destructive dynamic set in motion: we begin seeking out groups of people who will do nothing *but* affirm our bad ideas – and in so doing, place ourselves far beyond correction and growth, and into an endless cycle of error (and, in practice, social division). That's bad for us as individuals, bad for the group... bad for humankind.

What can be done about all this? Quite a bit.

To begin, we can each begin looking for the phenomenon within ourselves. Whenever we feel that surge of pleasure that comes from being told we are right, we can realize that this is really akin to a sugar high, and that it doesn't mean anything that's of value to us.
We then can begin taking caution with others, offering that affirmation only when we ourselves have done the due diligence on what our friend is putting forth. We often offer affirmation as an appeasement or a social lubricant; maybe we should rethink that.

Finally, we can consciously seek out social settings where affirmation is hard to come by – among people who will not automatically agree with us, where we have to put in some work and effort in order to receive it. We can decide to be in settings where affirmation of our ideas must be earned – where it cannot be contrived, gratuitous, or manipulative.

This is a lot of work, of course – but all forward motion is, in the end. It takes gargantuan effort to succeed as a species, to tune into the real world and respond to it in ways that promote our survival and growth. It is worthy work – and, of course, existentially unavoidable: The earth beneath us, after all, is littered with the remains of those who failed.

Ghosting

'Ghosting', the act of vanishing from a relationship without warning or explanation (any relationship - romantic, friendship, etc.), is on the increase. While common among millennials, it occurs among older people, too, and may be a disturbing consequence of all the new social connections we now cultivate across diverse media.

This strikes me as not only a deeply irresponsible way to live, but also unethical and perhaps even destructive. If, as Douglas Hofstadter has proposed, our personal identity is constructed from borrowed identity from those we are closest to, then the sudden and unexplained absence of a part of oneself could have a crippling, debilitating effect.

The more we study and discuss the social human, the more we realize that none of us is as autonomous as might be hoped: we are all deeply interconnected, and thoughts to the contrary are a conceit. Without the people we are close to, without the social systems we all lean on for support, the mind rapidly goes on vacation. And when a deeply-woven thread is suddenly yanked free, an unraveling may begin.

All of this is just to say - treat your relationships with a high degree of responsibility and accountability; they are a far more importance part of your life, of your self, than you might think.

How Will Our Worth Be Measured?

Anthropologists and other Paleo specialists like Robert Sapolsky have long since done the math: the effort required to sustain a human tribe in prehistory, once we achieved Cro-Magnon status, wasn't much. The creation and maintenance of tools to support a Cro-Magnon clan, spread across more than a hundred people, was the barest handful of hours per week; the hunting of fauna capable of meeting the calorie requirements of the tribe, along with the gathering of side dishes, amounted to less than 15 hours a week.

In short, human beings - because they are deeply social creatures who cooperate magnificently - are an order of magnitude more efficient than their gorilla cousins, or any other primates that spend 80-90 percent of their time pursuing food.

Today, of course, we require far more hours of labor per week in exchange for sustenance. We measure the worth of other human beings by their work output, casting aside all mitigating considerations.

The problem today: our technology is rapidly eroding our need to invest most of our time in work. Automation, a generation from now, will be performing 3/4ths of the work required to sustain human civilization. How, then, will our worth as human beings be measured?

"Against stupidity, the gods themselves contend in vain."

~Friedrich Schiller

Toxic

Some people are toxic.

This is a lesson we usually learn the hard way; it's not as if our parents or teachers pointed them out as we were growing up ("Stay away from Billy! He's toxic!"), and it's not as if there are any obvious criteria by which we recognize a toxic person.

We can't spot them ahead of time because toxicity between people is a relative thing. Oh, it's obvious in some cases, yes: when a friend breaks away from a highly manipulative, narcissistic other, an other with a history of failed manipulative relationships, it's easy to point to that narcissistic other and say "Toxic!" and accept it as a generality.

But by and large, the people in our lives who we can look back on and think of as toxic were toxic *to us* - not necessarily toxic in general. Yes, we failed with them, but some other person is as happy as can be; yes, we couldn't get along with them at work, but now they're part of an effective team.

It's often hard to admit, when looking back at a toxic relationship, that the other person was just bad for us, not just bad; that they aren't flawed, and we aren't really a victim, we were just in the wrong place at the wrong time with the wrong person. Such relationships are everywhere, not just with romantic partners; they occur in friendship, in the workplace, anywhere human beings are required to personally invest in one another.

And we want the other person, in that soured relationship, to be the wrong one. We want to be exonerated, to believe that we ourselves are in no way toxic. And that, of course, can never be as fully true as we would like.

Many of us our blessed, after a toxic relationship, with a strong and healthy one - a connection that is encouraging, enabling, empowering - and this success, with all its warm results, fills us with a sense of validation and affirmation. When we love someone or care for someone who loves or cares for us in return, we feel as good about ourselves as we feel about them. And this makes the past relationship seem all the more dysfunctional.

But it's important to admit that this is not necessarily so; our negative judgments of those left behind and our generous acquittals of self are an emotional balm, but often faux: the truth of human relationships is that they conform to the same rules and demonstrate the same weaknesses as we observe in our social group interaction. Every human being has differences in the brain, and consequently in the mind and heart, that they did not choose and for which they are not accountable. We seldom make allowance for the fact that these differences, which by and large we can't (or at least never learn how to) control, lead us into errors in understanding - and, in the end, a collapse of empathy.

That collapse of empathy leaves us feeling hurt, betrayed, suspicious, and is the source of that toxicity that sends us in another direction. But underneath it, we most often find, not betrayal or enmity or rancor, but only... difference.

And that's something we can work with.

To: The Left

Re: Your Anger

Dear Left,

Your anger is strong. Your anger is growing. Your anger has come to lead
your every word and action in these contentious, uncertain times.
Your anger isn't helping.

It's not that it is unjustified; you've been cheated. Those who have inspired
your anger have certainly earned it. They have taken from you one of your
most precious possessions - your voice. They are tossed aside your most
earnest offering - your trust. They are stealing from you, and from your
children, your greatest asset - your future.

You've been cheated. And now, on a daily basis, you are lied to. You are
treated like children, by leaders who seem unable to *not* act like children.
You have endured years of this dishonesty, this endless re-mortgaging of
your society by ideological banksters; you have put up with decades of
despicable insults, listening to an endless stream of hostility leveled at those
in your ranks, for the unpardonable sin than standing against the toxic
flood of Authoritarian incursion.

You were patient, you played fair. You used your voice as the Framers
empowered you to, and your fair play was exploited to the fullest. You
have every right to be angry.

You've watched as those who lack your power and station, those more
vulnerable, are not only attacked perpetually with aggressive abandon, as
though it is somehow natural they be reduced to something less than
human, as though their rights never were; as decades of tireless efforts to
preserve and defend those rights have been swept away by the fountain
pens of the Authoritarian; as they have been blamed for everything from
trade deficits to hurricanes, taunted by schoolyard bullies who see them as
easy lunch money marks. And it has made you angry.

You have every right to be angry.

But your anger is getting you nowhere. Your anger is itself a toxin. Your anger isn't helping.

Your anger is robbing you of attention. And the complexities of the assault on your way of life and your rights and your identity and your future demand, and will demand even more, every scrap of attention you can muster, if you're to curb that assault.

Your anger is robbing you of cognition. The effort to mute your say in the world, to lock you into servitude to your self-appointed betters, to constrain your choices, requires and will require even more your clarity of thought and decision and sustained problem-solving energy; "Stop the Right!", as a goal, is effective only as self-defense; it is not effective in solving those problems the Right is exploiting.

Your anger is robbing you of unity. The anger that has set the Right against itself, through almost 30 years of endless drive-time hostility and fear-mongering and pursuit of ideological purity, has spread from them to you; it is now the Left that is now factionalizing itself to shreds, infighting like never before, smearing and sabotaging its own to the detriment of all.

"But I'm entitled to my anger!" Yes, you are; but do you really want to trade it in for meaningful action? Or will you clutch it like Linus's blanket as you continue to be marginalized, as your peers are demonized, as your rights and voice are diluted, and your children's future is traded away?

"But my anger focuses and mobilizes me!" Really? To do what? To repost memes with greater intensity? To rail against the GOP more loudly? To watch SNL more faithfully? What are you *really* doing to change things?

There are only a handful of reasons for which anger evolved in mammals, and none of them apply to you. You have a problem - a very serious problem, a very serious *series* of problems. They demand your full attention; they demand your problem-solving best; they demand your most durable group unity. Your anger is weakening all of these within you and those with whom you commiserate.

Close your eyes. Take a deep breath. Let your anger go. And get to work...

"There is no passion to be found playing small – in settling for a life that is less than the one you are capable of living."

~Nelson Mandela

Believing Things That Are Not True

I will die believing some things that are not true, and this is a source of distress for me.

I was raised Fundamentalist, and at an early age I began to sense something wasn't right in the words and actions and thoughts of the social group in which I was deeply embedded. Across decades, I sorted it all out, and now I stand free - and apart from some old friends and family members, sadly.

The more I realized I was called upon to believe (and act upon) things I knew to be untrue, the more important it became to me to pursue what was real and true, and to refuse to be drawn in by groupchant. That's a long road and a long story, but it raises a new question:

Is a life that is lived in illusion, according to things that are not true, a wasted life?

Is time invested in fantasy notions of human nature and wrong beliefs about others time wasted?

Is a life lived in suspicion of other human beings a life of missed opportunity?

In the end, I can only decide for myself, and my decision, made long ago, was to get to the bottom of these issues. I think I've made some progress, but of course, there's still a long way to go.

But this I know: the embrace of a bad or wrongheaded idea, even if benign, robs me of the opportunity to embrace a good one; an assumption about others that keeps me at a distance from them, even if innocuous, robs me of the chance to know them. And acting upon bad ideas or bad information, when my actions impact others, makes me less a positive agent in the world and may lead me to diminish others.

My life is more than halfway spent. I may never root out all the wrong ideas that live in my mind, but by ceaselessly searching them out and leaving them behind, I improve both my quality of life and my potential to add value to the lives of others.

And there will be less wasted time...

Assumptions

Each human being carries within a full set of assumptions about self and others, a frame of human nature that was inherited from parents or peers or family or social tribe. These frames are taken for granted, as they are with us from early childhood and seldom challenged until adulthood.

All of our social behaviors and reactions to other people and groups are derived from those assumptions. *All* of our thinking about self and personal circumstance and potential future derive from those assumptions. *All* of our perspective on partnering, parenting, friendship and social obligation derive from those assumptions.

Most of those assumptions, given to us in childhood, came from religion or some other patriarchal hierarchy. *Most* of those assumptions paint human beings as naturally selfish, deceitful, hostile and violent. And thus begins a self-fulfilling prophecy that is now 500 generations old.

If those assumptions are bullshit – if we can replace them with a more objective, natural, scientific understanding of what human beings really are – then we can get out of the tar pit we're now trapped in, and continue to evolve…

"Uncivilised writing is writing which attempts to stand outside the human bubble and see us as we are: highly evolved apes with an array of talents and abilities which we are unleashing without sufficient thought, control, compassion or intelligence."

~The Dark Mountain Project

A Quick Sandwich

So I duck out for a quick sandwich, and I have in my hand Elaine Morgan's *The Scars of Evolution*.

And the guy who takes my order (!) tries to pick a fight, informing me that "evolution is just a theory!"

When someone says, "Evolution is just a theory!", they are saying (among other things), "I don't know what 'theory' means!" and "I don't understand scientific method!" and, very probably, "I can't spell 'hypothesis!'

And this opens up an even bigger hole in public discourse about the nature of human beings and the world: Rejection of a shared frame within which to discuss those natures that doesn't favor the perspective of any specific social group not only doesn't move the discourse forward - it makes real discourse flat-out impossible.

I smiled at the guy and answered, "Yes, it really is!" He took that to be agreement - when it was, of course, exactly the opposite.

Feel, Think, Act

Once upon a time, we had no cortex.

We had a limbic system, and that was it. This was long, long before we were mammals, let alone primates – but we know it to be true, because that limbic system is still in there, chugging away, day in and day out. Our cortex – a much more modern component of our brains – exists not to replace our limbic system, but to respond to it. To regulate it.

The limbic system is, if we can oversimply a bit, our emotional drive. But in its primitive state, we can think of it as something more - our original decision-making system (because *sans* cortex, it's all the decision-making system there is).

Many creatures of the earth still live this way: their limbic systems – their emotional responses to the world – guide their behavior, and this serves them well enough that they survive and thrive. Feel, act. Feel, act. It works.

But when we get to mammals, and especially the higher forms of them, to feel is not enough; our particular bodies in our particular environment required adaptive behavior. We couldn't take to the air, we couldn't retreat into the earth; we needed to behave strategically, concocting complex responses in the moment. Our diets were protein-rich, we grew a little more brain tissue, and a little more, and a little more, and that tissue adapted to meet that strategic challenge.

No longer was it Feel, Act. Life became Feel, *Think*, Act.
And as we moved toward our hominid state, and then dropped to two legs, that *Think* step grew and grew. And grew. And grew.

In evolutionary terms, it was a fast catch-up; we'd been feeling and acting for literally millions of years. *Thinking* has been around, in protracted terms, for less than five percent of our total existence.

And eventually we began spending as much time thinking as we do feeling and acting. And because thinking sits much higher in our overall awareness than feeling, we fool ourselves into thinking it's our whole decision-making system – when that limbic system is still in there, just like it's always been, chugging away day in and day out.

Feeling is the trigger of thought, and thought is the trigger of action. This is how our brains work, and this is the reality of how we function in the world. But in the faux universe we've created, we have the freedom and space and safety to mangle that reality, to gunk up our brainworks by failing to correctly evaluate, let alone understand, let alone respond appropriately to those things in the world which stir our emotions in the first place.

Setting aside that most of the things we respond to emotionally are contrived, and that a lot of the stirring is manipulation by others, there's the fact that we don't all have the *same* limbic systems.

As I move through my day, I will have passive emotional responses to all sorts of things, and they will inspire various thoughts, and some of those thoughts will lead me to act.

But the guy who works next to me has a somewhat different limbic system; it is not entirely unlike mine, but there are nuanced variations in what triggers his passive emotions. Different things comfort him, different things disturb him. Different things entertain him, different things appeal to him. And those different emotions inspire different thoughts. And his different thoughts lead to different actions.

Understanding this, we see ourselves and the rest of the human race in an entirely different light. For one thing, we begin to tap into the astonishing variety of inner human life, and can be led to awe at the potential of our species, when we realize how magnificent that diversity of thought can lead us to be – far, far greater in sum than we can ever be alone.

More importantly, it shines a harsh light on our ferocious criticism of one another: it seems ludicrous to be so disapproving of my neighbor's actions when I fully grasp that he's thinking very different thoughts, which he's coming by honestly, via his perfectly natural – and somewhat different – emotions.

This is not to say that there aren't actions and behaviors in others that are worthy of disapproval. Of course there are. But it is to say that the condescension of heaping moral judgments upon those who think and act differently is disingenuous at best – and self-deceptive, at worst. And neither serves to improve either our neighbor's behaviors or our own response to it.

We developed cortical decision-making – thought – as a means of pausing in the world, and in pausing we devise superior responses to it. We don't just react, as our distant lizard cousins do – we *stop and think*. That power to *stop and think* has led us to this astounding moment in the march of life when we, as autonomous creatures, actually understand how we work inside.

Now if we could only act on that…

"In locomotion by land… our progress has been most stupendous – surpassing all previous steps since the creation of the human race. In the days of Adam, the average speed of travel, if Adam ever did such things, was four miles an hour; in the year 1828, or *4,000 years afterwards, it was still only ten miles*, and sensible and scientific men were ready to affirm and eager to prove that this rate could never be materially exceeded; - in 1950 it is habitually forty miles an hour, and *seventy* for those who like it."

~The Economist

A Bug's Life

E.O. Wilson notes that human beings are part of one of the smallest clubs in the kingdom of life. We are a *eusocial* species – one with the nearly-unique trait of sacrificing some measure of personal reproductive potential in order to facilitate the greater goal of group survive[2].

Wilson notes, with some fascination and astonishment, that only 20 such species have been discovered thus far. And with the exception of a crustacean or two and a mole-rat, all the rest besides us are… insects.

Eusociality is the highest, most sophisticated level of social organization, making a specious largely impervious to the forces that might lead to extinction. Eusocial insect colonies, it is certain, will outlast Homo sapiens by hundreds of millions of years, even projecting our best possible species outcomes. What is curious is how we, upright mammals, have come to achieve this heightened state of being, which is largely the province of bugs.

Eusocial species are master cooperators. They are hyper-efficient food gatherers, rabid self-defenders, astonishingly skilled at all the components of survival. Their division of labor is brilliant, highly effective. And they take an extra evolutionary step that bolsters their group survival even more: they care for one another's young.

The role of cooperation in the evolutionary story has been under study for some time - but it is not as well-understood as the role competition, for a simple reason: Nature provides far fewer examples of it. Among many species, it's every creature for itself; among many, it's just a travel buddy thing; even among mammals, many peacefully share territory, but the daily business of eating and sleeping and reproducing isn't considered group activity. It's far more common to see competition, aggression, fighting and fleeing and so on than it is to see the well-ordered community of an insect colony.

---

[2] Some biologists contest Wilson's assertion, noting that the other eusocial species all have reproductive and non-reproductive divisions of labor; Wilson counters that this division need not be absolute, but can be a matter of degree.

Here's the thing: if we look at cooperation as the antithesis of competition, we realize something unsettling: *without* their magnificent cooperation, eusocial insects would be astonishingly vulnerable.

They would be individually much weaker, much more fragile, much more exposed – much less able to draw sustenance from the world. And that's not the unsettling part…

…so would we.

An individual human being alone in the world is orders of magnitude more vulnerable than a human in a clan of humans. We are far slower than most other mammals. We are not armed with claws or fangs. We can no longer climb as we once did.

And the ingenuity we innately feel in the here-and-now? That's a heritage from hundreds of thousands of years of ingenuity, handed to us by… the group. Without it, we would flounder in the wild.

But put human beings into eusocial groups, and… *wow.* One human against a leopard is cat food. Six humans against a leopard, the leopard is the food.

Moreover, our infant survival rate skyrockets when we bind into large families. Out in the wild, adoption is rare: most infants will die if their parents die. Among humans, that almost never happens.

And that we care for one another's young has led us to care for one another; we have a power transcending all other eusocial species – empathy. When another of our kind hurts, we hurt; when another feels pleasure, we feel pleasure.

It is not a great leap to see that cooperation is more than just an alternative to competition – it is the next step. Having jumped species, from insect to primate, cooperation can now take Life where competition could not.
It falls to us now, to choose the one over the other. It falls to us now, to choose the one over the other.

Play Ball!

The Big Team Baseball Owners were not happy, and gathered together to commiserate.

"The problem," said the Owner of the Yankees, "is these damn 'sabermetrics'! Now we've got those paupers in Oakland fielding a team almost as skilled and entertaining as my Bronx Bombers, for one-third the price! It ain't right."

"The handwriting is on the wall," said the Owner of the Dodgers. "Oakland has changed the game, and for the worse. No longer is baseball about summer days and handsome pitchers and powerhouse hitters. Now even the poverty-ridden franchise can hire a smart young Harvard statistics major and win twenty games in a row."

"Boys," said the Owner of the Red Sox, "If the game has changed, it seems to me the rules need to change, as well – or we will lose our well-deserved stature."

"Wait a minute," said the Owner of the Giants. "What are we talking about here? So Oakland ups their game and brings in new talent – so what? Isn't that a good thing?"

"It's about the bottom line," said the Owner of the Dodgers. "They put together a pennant-worthy first-year line-up with less money than any of us could have managed. They're too damn efficient! We don't need the competition."

"But baseball is *about* competition," said the Owner of the Giants. "Healthy competition is the entire point of sports, and it's what the public loves about us! We can't take steps to diminish competition – it wouldn't be healthy, not for us or for the sport or for the fans!"

Chuckles around the table.

"We have enough trouble competing with each other," said the Owner of the Yankees. "We have one thing Oakland doesn't have – the power to do something about it. And we will."

"Are you talking about...?" The Owner of the Giants felt a lump in his throat.

"Changing the rules," said the Owner of the Dodgers: *"Deregulation."*

So the Big Team Owners went to the Commissioner and shared their thinking, and did not invite the Owner of the Giants along. When the Commissioner did not like their thinking, they bought themselves a new Commissioner, because they could, and the new Commissioner was far more agreeable.

The rule that said One Team Cannot Own Another Team was struck down. Immediately, the As, the Padres, the Brewers and the Pirates were bought up, their star players retained and the rest dismissed, and their stadiums re-branded.

So well did this work that the Big Team Owners got together again, having replaced the Owner of the Giants with the much more entrepreneurial Owner of the Tigers.

"Boys," said the Owner of the Yankees, "these goddamn free agents are killing us! Ardolis Chapman kicked my ass!"

"And Rich Hill kicked mine," said the Owner of the Dodgers. "We gotta talk to the Commish."

So the Big Team Owners went back to their Commissioner, who made a new rule that it was okay for them to agree upon salary caps and impose them across both Leagues.

This, too, worked out great: now their year-to-year fortunes would no longer be tied to the contractual caprices of the fickle pretty boys, with their whimsical demands and their elitist endorsement deals.

Meanwhile, they gobbled up the Braves, the Reds, the Phillies and the Indians.

In the dictionary, under Too Good to Be True, one might expect a selfie of the Big Team Owners. Now, the sky was the limit.

"I'm not happy with turnout," said the Owner of the Red Sox at their next meeting. "The crowds just aren't what they used to be."

"It's the stadiums," said the Owner of the Tigers. "We need to incentivize them to bring in more people."

"But how?" asked the Owner of the Dodgers.

"I have an idea," said the Owner of the Yankees. And off they went to the Commissioner.

A quick flick of the pen, and the Big Team Owners forced a renegotiation with their home cities, requiring that their contracts for their home stadiums include the bundling of season football tickets with season baseball tickets – at premium prices, agreed upon between them.

And they quietly absorbed the Mets, the Angels, the Orioles and the Cubs.

So easy was it for their teams to win, at this point, that their players had stopped training – or staying fit at all. Many gained weight, and as their skills atrophied, the Owners propped up ticket sales by turning to spectacle – uniforms with gold and silver lamé inset, robot battles on the field between innings, live rock bands in place of the traditional organ.

The Owner of the Giants crashed the next meeting.

"Do you realize what you've done?" he wailed with authentic dismay. "You've turned healthy competition into *anti*-competition! There's no trace of baseball left, no real red-blooded American ballgame left!"

"You're confusing *competing* with *winning*," grinned the Owner of the Yankees, "and we are most definitely winning! We just had our biggest year ever, and there's no end in sight."

"Oh, yeah?" the Owner of the Giants defiantly shot back. "Play my guys! Exhibition game! The four of you are just about the only teams left – pick your very best players, put them on the field, and my solitary Giants will mop them up!"

The Big Team Owners were not about to do that, of course. Instead, they forced the Giants out of business by refusing to permit *any* Major League team to play them. The Commissioner remained silent.

Finally, it was just the Yankees and the Dodgers, who had let all the players' contracts expire and had backfilled those pricy uniforms with cheap foreign actors. All the stadiums were branded Y or D (with rotating sponsors), and the games were tightly scripted.

The Owner of the Yankees and the Owner of the Dodgers sat together, having a beer.

"I do miss the old days," said the Owner of the Dodgers. "I can't remember the last game I saw where I didn't know ahead of time who was going to win."

"Ah, but you don't miss the headaches, do you?" said the Owner of the Yankees. "The old Commissioners, free agents, dealing with city councils, negotiating with the networks – we run the table now. And you're 100 times richer than you were!"

"Still," ruminated the Owner of the Dodgers, "there's something to be said about the simplicity of this business as it was before... good years, bad years... uncertain outcomes... Monday night television... five-dollar hot dogs..." He yawned. "This game has a soul. Koufax on the mound. The Babe at the plate."

"That's what we tell the rubes who pay the bills," winked the Owner of the Yankees, "but we know better, eh?"

"What do you mean?"

"The soul of this game, of any game, is a commodity," said the Owner of the Yankees. "It's never been about *what* the people pay to watch – it's just making sure they keep watching, and keep paying to watch. That's why we had to get out from under those pesky regulators! We weren't free to innovate!"

He lit a cigar. "'Competition,'" he sneered, puffing big. "Competition is for track stars and beauty queens! We've taken baseball and made it *truly* American – a new and creative business model! And that, my friend, is what's American about it."

He exhaled. "...as American as apple pie!"

Mother Nature Doesn't Care

Mother Nature doesn't care where your anger and rage are coming from.

There is no difference, brain-wise, in the faux rage of the Trump Voter who is all jacked up from something s/he heard on Talk Radio or what the fire-breather in the pulpit said, and the righteous rage of the frustrated Bernie-voting social justice warrior.

The human brain is, ironically, indifferent to the *source* of your rage, which is contrived, abstract and wholly social in origin in both cases. The brain will raid your reasoning center and your attention facility, in equal measure, no matter what inspired your ire.

The Left Leaner, then, becomes as deficit in the tools need to bring about meaningful change as the Right Leaner, for exactly the same reasons: when we indulge in anger and rage and self-righteous justification of either, we diminish those powers which enable the richness of our social universe in the first place.

Put another way – if you hope to make a difference, no matter where your anger is coming from -dial it down.

"The Agricultural Revolution certainly enlarged the sum total of food at the disposal of humankind, but the extra food did not translate into a better diet or more leisure. Rather, it translated into population explosions and pampered elites. The average farmer worked harder than the average forager, and got a worse diet in return. The Agricultural Revolution was history's greatest fraud."

~Yuval Noah Harari

Cognitive Bigotry

There is racial diversity, there is cultural diversity - and there is *cognitive* diversity.

Human beings vary widely in physical appearance. We come in all shapes, sizes, and colors. We vary widely culturally - where you come from determines who you are, to a great deal, and the places we come from likewise vary widely.

But we also differ - and far more deeply and significantly - in how our brains work. Different parts of the human brain do different jobs, in boosting us through our lives and navigating the world, and the variations in those parts mean variations in how we process the world, ourselves, and each other.

This cognitive diversity is by far the most influential, consequential, and ultimately important of all human diversities. Wide variation in skin color isn't even noticed, until humans travel great distances and leave their geographical regions; ditto cultural diversity, which only matters when we step away from our own homeland.

But cognitive diversity exists *within* our region, *within* our homeland - inevitably, since it is delivered by our genes; and essentially, since it is our cognitive diversity that gives us the problem-solving bandwidth to transcend those threats that have dogged us and risen up against us through the eons.

Until now.

Now, it's a very different world. Now, we segregate not only by skin color, not only by culture - but by cognitive type.

Our cognitive type - our social behavioral dispositions that derive from our personal neurochemistry - are defined by some of our core emotional responses and biases: how easily are we frightened or threatened? How exploratory are we? How sensitive to change? Do we prefer to be led, or do we prefer to live by consensus? Our personal answers to these questions define the path by which we, as individuals, engage the world.

And in this whacked social universe we've built, we are more segregated, in cognitive diversity terms, than the US South ever was, racially - or the Middle East, culturally - or Europe, religiously.

And it is the diversity proponents, the anti-segregation crowd - the Left - that has the most to answer for.

It's one thing to be cognitively predisposed to be more fearful of outsiders than normal, to be raised among in-kind others, and become an adult who conforms to the faux boundaries of physical and cultural difference. It is something very different to be free of such chains, to have an abundance of tolerance and a heart for both diversity and social justice - and then leap into the Bigotry Pool with a 10-year-old's cannonball form, shouting, "Repuglican! Deplorable!" with all the energy of a Little Rock protester shouting "Nigger bitch!" or a Westboro pew-sitter hollering "Faggot!" or a talk radio blowhard bellowing "Slut!"

We don't choose the predispositions of our social cognition any more than we choose our gender, our skin color or our sexual orientation. When you stand before an Authoritarian voter who clutches the flag and abhors those who look different and goes to church five times a week, you can think and feel what you please - but Science (which you ostensibly favor) bids you realize, 'There, but for the random tumble of the genetic dice, stand I.'

This is not to say - by *any* means! - that the bad ideas or unhealthy actions of those who hover in another cognitive domain should be given a free pass, or that tolerance should extend to group-justified abuses from any quarter. These things should be energetically opposed, regardless of source, from without or within.

But opposing socially destructive attitudes and behaviors, and entertaining anger and disdain for those who see the world and themselves and other human beings differently are not the same thing at all. The first is the social check-and-balance that keeps human beings moving through history, against the indifferent forces of life on earth, as one..

The latter is scornful bleat of the playground bully, a force opposing not only our progress but our well-being, corrosive to the human spirit. It is bigotry, pure and simple - and it has no place in the Human Story, period. It needs to stop, wherever we can find the will.

Uncle Scott's Handy Guide to Bigotry/Diversity

Lots of stuff flying through the air these days, in the bigotry domain, right? Hatred of Muslims, hatred of gays, hatred of women, hatred of Trump voters - all flying hither and yon, 24/7, on Facebook, on Twitter, on cable news. Everywhere! Look out! Duck!

Then there's the other side of the coin - the anti-bigots, those who want to see an end to the screech of the intolerant: they want to live in a calmer, more welcoming world, a society that is inclusive and celebrating of difference.

In both cases, it's about difference. And this is where it gets squirrelly! What counts as a difference we can use to exclude others? What counts as a difference to be recognized and celebrated?

Your Uncle Scott is here to help you sort it all out, with this handy-dandy guide!

Physical Differences! These are, by far, the most basic of triggers for bigotry. If another person has skin of a different color, *bing*! If you're a bigot, you're home already - this person is different from me, someone I can safely categorize as an Other from the outset. Runners up: Women, with those bumps and curves and vacancies that signal, right away, Other-ness!; The Handicapped, who make me uncomfortable just by moving around differently; and, of course, Old People.

And all of these physical traits are, of course, easy flags for the Diversiphile, who needs to come alongside and defend.

Behavioral Differences! Physical differences give the bigot an easy leg up, in hunkering down and defining their tribe. A bit trickier is knowing who to exclude, in that group of people who do NOT look different.
Pinning down Otherness is not so easy, when the Other looks just like me! These targets must be observed carefully for those markers that set them apart.

Did you see that guy? He just hugged another man! Must be gay! Other! ---
easier and easier, as homosexuals creep out of their closets. And that little
guy with the beard, he goes to church on Saturday, at that funny place that
doesn't have crosses on it: Jew!

And the Diversiphile is right there, homing in on the same signals, ready to
wear a supportive rainbow pin or acknowledge the Holocaust.

Now the bigot is scrambling hard, to continue winnowing down the tribe.
What about those who look the same and don't have overtly different
behaviors - those differences that aren't physical or behavioral, but simply
differences in thought?

Cognitive Differences! Now, at long last, the differences between us are
utterly undetectable on the street: at the mall, at the ball game, in the
elevator, I can't know if the person standing next to me is tribe-worthy or
not without extensive dialog. I need to probe their 'beliefs,' their point of
view, learning what's important to them in order to know whether they are
enough like me or not to be worthy of my approval/scorn.

This level of difference is simultaneously too shallow to inspire deep
scrutiny and too deep to be scrutinized by any but the most committed, on
either the bigot or diversiphile sides of the street. Realizing that not
everyone thinks the same way is a tough enough hurdle (a boon for the
bigot!); understanding that these differences are not moral discriminators,
but physiological traits we do not choose is tougher still (a boon for the self-
righteous progressive!)

Put another way, cognitive differences are so subtle, compared to skin color
and genuflections, that they put up no struggle against the bigot, and offer
the tolerant an easy off-ramp, when tolerance becomes strenuous.

To be accepting, not only of those who look differently and behavior
differently, but *think* differently, is a place for only the most dedicated, kind,
and accepting among us - no place for snowflakes. You have to *work* to truly
embrace human diversity, if you're to be this open and inclusive - and that
only happens, as pointed out above, when we take the extra step of entering
into meaningful dialog with that Maybe-Other, learning their worldview
and exploring the differences between our ideas and theirs.

And, as *Star Trek's* Q once said, *It's not safe there! It's wondrous, with treasures to satiate desires both subtle and gross - but it's not for the timid...*

Getting Choosy!

Recently I started feeling that it was time for a change.

I can't tell you what change I was needing, mind you, but I was overcome with a general sense of restlessness, that nagging need for something *new* in my life – and I just had this feeling that it's time to mix it up.

What to change? Now that's a puzzle. Time to give up briefs for boxers? Give up *Star Trek* reruns? Dr. Pepper? Captain Crunch?

I turned to the Internet for wisdom. Always a good choice!

Change is not so tough, I read; if you want to change, all you have to do is *decide* to change! All of life, I read, was defined by our choices – and nothing in life is un-choose-able. I was, frankly, *amazed* at some of the things that are matters of choice!

I opted to approach the matter of life-change slowly, experimentally – to test out this theory of choosy-ness a little at a time, to see 1) if it was true, and 2) how far it could go.

I saw in some memes on Facebook that I could change my beliefs by simply deciding to - both Right and Left seem to agree that people believe what they believe because they *choose* to. Hmm... is it that simple? I can't really remember when I decided to believe the things I believe – I always thought those believes built up inside me over time, assembled from my experience and the things I saw and heard and lived through – and there came a moment when each of my beliefs began to choose *me*, not the other way around.

Still – what do I know? How could I be smarter than the Internet?

I started out small. What did I believe in? What, among those things I believe in, was I willing to change?

Hm, well, I believe in social justice; I believe it's self-evident that all men (and women) are created equal; I believe that we should feed the hungry and care for the sick. People tell me this makes me 1) a liberal, and 2) not a Christian. Okay. I decided to stop being a liberal. If I *chose* to be a liberal to begin with, then I could simply *choose* to be a conservative.

It worked!!!

In the blink of an eye, I suddenly realized that our priority is to protect ourselves in a dangerous world; that public assistance for the sick and the old makes them dependent; that inequality is a natural consequence of freedom!

I believed these things with all my heart, *in the blink of an eye!* It really was that easy!

We simply *choose* our beliefs! We can un-choose them!

Armed with this success, I bumped it up a notch.

My beliefs about providing for the sick and hungry, social justice and equality had kept me from the church. I had shed these beliefs, now, but somehow I didn't feel that this was the same as choosing my religion. So I decided to actually *choose*.

I have long maintained, when confronted by Evangelicals, that while I cannot *prove* there is no such entity as the Jewish deity Yahweh, I *can* prove that the likelihood of Yahweh existing is equal to the likelihood that of the Greek God Zeus existing. All of these being equal, then, I found some dice, rolled them – and chose the Norse God Odin.

It worked, by Odin!

Suddenly I felt awash with Odin's mighty presence, trembling with awe – a vast rainbow stretched into the sky, and I felt the overwhelming urge to jump in a big wooden boat!

And if I could change *that* belief...

It was time to go All In.

I remembered the faith of my childhood – that innocent, earnest respect and passion and deep longing that drew me to some of my peers, set me apart from others... that one belief that had defined me from boyhood to the present day.

I closed my eyes, clenched my fists, ready to say "Farewell!" to that belief and embrace a new one.

And that quickly, I no longer loved the Dallas Cowboys. Now I was a Green Bay man.

I googled Tom Landry and gazed at his mature visage, his calm demeanor, his quiet strength, and... nothing. I was unmoved. It was Aaron Rodgers for me, from this day forward.

Okay, now we're cooking! I considered taking the next step – in for a penny, in for a pound!

If I could change my mind... could I change the rest of me? Could my *physical* preferences change, just by choosing?

Brussel sprouts make me vomit. Always have, since Thanksgiving at Grandma's in 1968. The Facebook memes I had seen told me that my physical desires are *choices*, not actual physical responses of my senses and brain – so that meant I could change what my body wants and needs just by thinking it, right?

I bought some Brussel sprouts in the frozen foods section, took them home, and cooked them up in butter. Then I *chose* to love them.

By Odin's Beard! They were wonderful!!!

And if *that* was true...

...then everything the Right and the Fundies had been saying all this time about you-know-what being a choice was true.

I had *chosen* to like girls!

I remember well my 12th year, at Darlington Junior High School. I remember the jukebox in the corridor next to the gym, and that day when I'd walked right into Shari Nichols and almost knocked her down, and how she had smiled and said, "Excuse me!" and I had forgotten my mother tongue and almost passed out. And how I'd written her name 75 times on a piece of notebook paper that day in study hall.

All these years, who knew? I had *chosen* to be attracted to Shari Nichols!

What a waste! In the decades sense, I have walked into so many clubs and parties, and in any large group of females – all of whom might have been considered at least nominally attractive – I'd find myself drawn, with no forethought, toward one in particular. I'd always thought of this attraction, this *type* of woman who beckoned to my particular desires, to be a consequence of my personal sexual chemistry – my customized mix of hormones and experience and genes.

But if I could choose...

I went to the mall. I found a bench and sat. Immediately I was drawn to an attractive blonde – my lifelong preference. And I'm an ass man, satisfied with midrange boobs but loving a great rear view!

I closed my eyes, thought Big-Boobed Brunette... and *voila!*

That quickly, I lost all interest in the blonde, and rapidly homed in on a buxom brown-haired beauty in heels with an oversized handbag.

And if I could choose *that...*

I had to know.

The memes say it's a choice. The Evangelical preachers say it's a choice. *Fox News* says it's a choice!

I closed my eyes once again, and chose... *guys.*

Suddenly, all the women in the mall vanished, as far as I was concerned. None held any interest whatsoever! But... *wow!* When it came to the guys – a smorgasbord!

Over there, a tall, handsome frat boy with an ass as tight as a snare drum –
and over there, a bald hunk in jeans who looks like he could bench twice his
body weight! And over there, the one with the sandy-blond hair and electric
smile...

And my new-found appreciation of Aaron Rodgers grew even more!
I couldn't take it anymore! Time to call this a *huge* success, it turns out we
can *choose* our preferences! Our needs and desires are just a matter of
choice! All this fretting over our differences and biology and equality – all
just political posturing, after all!

Embracing this newfound freedom, letting go of all that untidy intellectual
baggage, I arose from the bench in the mall, reveling in my new self, and
headed home – to watch *Outlander*...

Trigger Fingers

Robert Altemeyer, the congenial Canadian psychologist who has led the world's research on Authoritarianism, sought to understand social aggression – the systematic heaping of hostility of one group onto another, a defining feature of our world.

Following up on physicist Steven Weinberg's famous quote about "getting good people to do evil things – that takes religion," he took his research into the behaviors of the Authoritarian Follower a few extra steps, asking the question, What makes otherwise calm and peaceful people aggressive against others?

It turns out to be a complex mix, and it took him many years. Working from his already-tested Authoritarian scale, he surveyed hundreds of high-Authoritarian subjects, and here's what he discovered:

Fear is the first essential ingredient in Authoritarian aggression. For an Authoritarian Follower to be moved to group violence against another group, they need to be fearful of those against whom they're aggressing.

This makes complete sense, because that's the evolutionary purpose of fear. But fear alone is clearly not enough; many if not most fearful people choose flight over fight – they simply avoid those who make them frightened or uncomfortable.

Altemeyer found the next peace – *Anger*. The difference, in the animal kingdom (and even more so in the world of humans) between the fearful who fight and the fearful who flee is anger. Fear centers attention on the object of our terror, and where anger is absent, we run; where anger is present, we aggress.

Even so, there are plenty of people who are afraid of others and feel constant, smoldering anger and resentment of those who are making us uncomfortable, yet never rise up against them. Altemeyer had not yet completed the equation.

Aggression is a social act, especially when one group rises up against another group. That remaining missing piece, he found, was a social trigger: moral superiority.

The social response of the Authoritarian Follower to those others who make them afraid and angry is to diminish their humanity, and in so doing, enhance their own. Self-righteousness – I am better than you! – achieves both: *I am better… more worthy… more entitled!* And in a group: *We are better… we are more worthy… we are more entitled!*

And now we have ourselves an Authoritarian ballgame. Brown shirts. A klan.

Our problem is this: the core triggers of aggression – fear and anger – are perfectly natural, and exist in *all* of us, to some degree. They've been with us for millions of years, and they're not going away anytime soon.
But thanks to Bob Altemeyer, we can now be pretty certain that *social* aggression hinges on that last component –self-righteousness. Without it, aggression is a smoldering ember, rather than a forest fire.

And that's something we *can* do something about. The nature of social groups, how they form and bond and behave, is increasingly well-understood, and a consequence of the value systems we've deployed in the world. How people feel about themselves – and how groups feel about other groups – follows from our social disbursements. If we want to disable and dispel moral superiority, we need to redefine what those words mean, and permeate the world with new and better examples. Hard to do, in such a frightened world – but not impossible. We lack only the will to make it happen.

The Orcs Are Coming!

They sprawl across floor and chair, as still as battlefield casualties, Yuletide meal vanquished, staring through a tryptophan haze as Mordor's slimy hordes advance menacingly on Aragorn's doughty band. We do this every Christmas, me and my assorted zygotes, pushing through all three extended-edition installments of The Lord of the Rings in one heroic advance, which requires a resolve not incomparable to that of Frodo himself.

And every year, as the Orcs advance, I do my pedantic riff on Tolkien's ham-handed substitution of leathery, hulkish sub-humans for the frightful German columns of his own none-too-real war, carefully pointing out that it is an ancient deceit of the powerful that our enemies are not as human as we ourselves. I caution them to be on the lookout, and they ignore me completely, weaving yet another warm family moment forever into our ritual tapestry.

If Tolkien's minions of darkness were ridiculously monochrome, at least his Middle Earth protagonists had a broad palette of delightful moral shadings. Tolkien's drinking buddy C.S. Lewis, on the other hand, populated his Narnia with biodiversity that would have Edward O. Wilson doing handsprings – and then pounded it all flat with a suffocating moral bivalence that made the Orcs look like a grad school philosophy study group.

This issue of shirts and skins is of great importance to me, or I would not continually risk being *shushed* by my kids over it. I want it to be important to them, not just so they'll be able to sort out which is which as the future unfolds, but in hopes of urging them away from other people's Othering of other people.

Holding hands on the hillside, showing love to your brother – your sister and your mother – but we hate those people down the valley! goes the Tull song. That's all this Othering stuff used to be about, back when we were all really hairy and ugly and way more Orcish. Pre-McDonald's, it was all about the food having a tendency to hide behind trees and run really fast, and having to go find it and catch it, and the tendency of the neighbors to grab it first. Safe to say that in those days everybody looked and smelled equally Orc-like; so

the only real difference, group to group, was who got the Big Mac.
Reason enough to Other the others, under the circumstances – and Othering
turns out to be a pretty effective alligator moat. *We hate those people down the
valley,* and each group steers clear, apart from occasionally borrowing each
Other's wimminfolk.

William Graham Sumner (1840-1910) gave us a new big word for this,
ethnocentrism – "the view of things in which one's own group is the center of
everything, and all Others are scaled and rated with reference to it
(capitalization mine)." In our Orcish days, one's own group *was* the center
of everything; but that was, you know, thirty thousand years ago. Today,
there's a Mickey D's on every corner – yet we're Othering each other more
than ever.

Sumner, making up the field of sociology as he went along, deftly
explicated the anthropological roots of this idea, placing it squarely on the
Natural Behavior shelf – then spent many years teasing out the social and
moral consequences. Judging everybody else based on our high opinions of
ourselves, he pointed out, leaves us with far more than bambi stew and
exotic wimminfolk; it gives us pride, vanity, superiority, and contempt. It's
natural and understandable that we do it, he said, but it arguably does us
far more harm than good, the world being what it is today.

Making matters worse, the Othering that gives us this moral bounty is,
historically, about Real Things: significant differences in behaviors between
groups and the meanings attached to behaviors, differences and meanings
that can only be negotiated by actively stepping into another viewpoint. But
Othering, it turns out, doesn't need to be about Real Things at all.

The ground-breaking innovation of pulling group differences out of thin
air, inventing ways of creating an Us/Them chasm right here in the middle
of Us, changed the Human Story forever. We developed the power to
reshape groups, split groups, and purge groups by just making things up,
and we learned that there was no limit to how finely the hair could be split.
We could do Broad and Obvious (Sci-Fi vs. Fantasy) to Fine Distinctions
(*Star Wars* vs. *Star Trek*) to Nobody Sees It and Nobody Cares (Old *Trek* vs.
New *Trek*). Making up new meanings for things opened up vast frontier
territories of behaviors: we could make up new reasons for doing old things
(killing everybody next door) and even think up new behaviors just to give
an invented meaning something to do (the amputation of foreskins).

And a power it truly has been. This whole invented-differences thing has, over the centuries, worked better than skin color and genitalia and relative wealth *combined*, in setting people against each other and getting them to do bad things. It's given us social structures that are able to flourish in almost any culture, under any political system, able to rally chanting thousands to oppose, and often slaughter, almost any Other its leaders designate. It can render the minds of its adherents impervious to reason, compassion, rule-of-law and independent moral judgment. It has produced, in particular, one meme-complex – an array of self-replicating, self-reinforcing concepts – that is for all practical purposes impenetrable. Or, more simply, "Religion".

But lest we swap horse for cart, let's remember that Religion is just one form (albeit the most notorious) of Othering, by far the broader and more ancient tradition. Othering itself can go places Religion can't; for instance, I can create a religion, join a religion, exclude Others from a religion – but I can't put anybody else *into* a Religion. Othering, on the other hand, can go there and beyond. I can be in this group or that, exclude Others from my group, and even invent a group to Other them into, whether they like it or not. If I'm the Pope, I can Other Others into all sorts of dubious groups – apostates, heretics, witches – but I can't Other another into a Religion.

Whew!

Well, this does complicate things. While it's a relief that I can't get Othered into an actual group I don't want to be in (except at gunpoint), it's still true that Others can Other me into some Other group that doesn't really exist, but which I don't want written on my underwear label, all the same.

Usually this takes some doing, as the Otherers scramble to invent some criteria with which to justify the Othering, which will include some overt misrepresentation, as in the racist's misrepresentation of blacks, conservatives' misrepresentation of liberals, and the Christian Right's misrepresentation of … well, everyone. (I myself get misrepresented with alarming regularity. Conservatives misrepresent me as a Liberal; Evangelicals misrepresent me as an Atheist; Freudians misrepresent me as a Jungian. How, exactly, is any Other made more distinct or secure by the sewing of exaggerated or blatantly invented labels into my jockey shorts?) To be sure, there is some Othering that is useful, or at least inevitable; there are, after all, groups of humans that are inarguably distinct in ways that derive from qualities or behaviors that they alone possess, or whose behaviors produce meaning that is clear and universal across cultures (The Beatles, the '69 Mets, Knights Who Say 'Ni'). But Othering is far more often about this group or that applying definitions to people with no interest in what they might think of it, or even the reality of it.

And the dangers of this Othering, returning to Sumner's moral consequences, are not something we can really work around. If we Other Others, we're going to be worse than morally compromised; we're going to be *wrong*, even when the boundaries are agreed upon and legitimate. Why? It turns out that the wrongness is built into our brains.

The ability to create categories and put things into them is a mental innovation that bolsters our memories. It's something we're really good at, and it works wonderfully, as far as that goes. But we have also learned, by way of research in cognitive psychology, that when we categorize things, *we have a strong tendency to overestimate the similarities* between things in one group, and to *overestimate the differences* of things in other groups. When we put things into groups, we no longer see them as clearly as we did before. Here's a fun example. If I present these groups of letters,

CHO,

PHO,

USE

and instruct someone to pronounce the word they form, most of the time they will say *"choh-foh-use!"* But remove the commas – eliminate the letter-"groups" – and a very different (and far more accurate) answer presents itself:

CHOPHOUSE

Now imagine how much worse things get, when it's people that have been comma'd apart. Who, in your own life, have you comma'd out?

We end up doing exactly what Tolkien did, reducing the humanity of those outside our circle. We end up missing important details that are too subtle to penetrate the cloud of misrepresentation. We no longer see actual people. In the extreme, we can repaint the entire world in the wrong colors and obscure most of what matters, as in the Christian Right's persistent impulse to Narniate an American landscape that's just about as Middle-Earthy as can be.

We end up seeing versions of each other – and, in the end, ourselves – that aren't real. We have a word for that, too: *fantasy*. Fine if you're Tolkien or Lewis, but in the real world? Not so much.

Othering, then, makes us both arbitrary and inaccurate – two things that bolster the resume, if you're a Fox News commentator, but are otherwise pretty undesirable. It does bolster the memory – but that seems less than compelling, in an era when most of us carry 100+ gigabytes of random-access storage in our shirt pockets.

On the other hand, if we can Other Others creatively for nefarious purposes, might we not also Other Others for constructive purposes? Can we imagine a future in which we invent groups into which we drop people based on their potential, or their as-yet-undeveloped contributions? Can we re-draw the boundaries around those who are already disenfranchised and despised, and see them in a new light? Can we leverage the anthropological twist of Sumner's ethnocentrism in ways that ennoble us?

Alas … only if we're all on the same page, and come to some social consensus that it's a good thing if we put everybody in some Other category that puts forth their better qualities?
Dare to dream …

They sprawl across floor and chair, and if I push it they'll only *shush* me, not that I know quite what to say anyway. What exactly is there to say? That the world is actually full of Orcs, endless hordes who really do wish them dead, for no better reason than that they live where they do, or that they don't say the right prayer to the right god, or that they have too many shoes.

That at the very least, people are going to be Othering them all their lives, hating or rejecting or excluding them for no good reason, and many of those who don't will frequently encourage them to join in the mindless, self-destructive, orgiastic pneumacide of Othering.

I want to tell them that there are really only two kinds of people in the world, those who wish them no harm and those who do; and I want to assure them that it's easy to tell which is which.

But … that turns out not to be the case.

EON Nation

Dr. Jerald Hughes of the University of Texas makes an interesting point regarding the cognitive style of the US Founding Fathers: the manner in which they constructed the United States, and the rules they set in motion for its operation, conform to their cognitive style – a style that is unified, easily clarified, and whose functionality is clear and consistent.

To begin with, it is an explicitly *egalitarian* style of thinking. Those populating the United States in its early decades were deliberately taking a stand against the authoritarian rule of both the Anglican Church and King George III – authoritarian rule that left them longing for both independence from autocracy and autonomy in government.

To this end, the Founders constructed a government that distributed authority in such a way that it could never be concentrated in any one person or group – and, moreover, distributed that authority as evenly as possible. The US hosts a purposely egalitarian government.

The New World, as it was called, was not just a bolt hole for escaping authority – it was, hyperbole aside, a Land of Opportunity. Untold riches in resources lay waiting to be discovered; a new form of government implied potential for a new social order, new possibilities in community-building; a new economy, as well as new international political and trading relationships, were all enabled by the act of the colonies seeking to become a new nation.

To this end, ordinary citizens were given unprecedented freedoms, and committed protection of those freedoms, by their government - to encourage participation and personal industry, an encouragement that made the United States the most prosperous, inventive nation in history.

Finally, the Founders were men with affinity for novelty, whose contentment with status quo was tenuous, when it existed at all – men willing to set aside old ways and pursue the new idea, to risk all on the never-before-tried. An entire continent lay before them, an endless landscape of discovery and challenge.

They met this challenge by aggressively supporting both exploration and expansion, encouraging westward expeditions and unfettered homesteading. The United States, for all its growing pains, flowered at many times the pace of its European antecedents, serving up the new and different Egalitarian, Opportunity-scanning, Novelty-seeking (EON): this was the cognitive template of the United States, taken from its Founders – each of which possessed these predispositions in bargeloads.
The problem is...

It is not possible, nor even practical, to sustain this cognitive paradigm as a template for a society, not even if the initial population is *entirely* EON.

Why? Because cognitive predispositions are based on the relative volume and connectivity of brain components, and those volumes and connectivities are genetically linked. Put another way, you can start out with half a million EONs, but within a generation or two, you'll have ETNs (Egalitarian/Threat-scanning/Novelty-seeking) and AONs (Authoritarian/Opportunity-scanning/Novelty-seeking) and EOUs (Egalitarian/Opportunity-scanning/Uniformity-seeking) and ATUs, (you get the idea) and so on, aplenty. *No* population can remain a representation of a single cognitive style over time.

Moreover, we shouldn't ever want it to: cognitive diversity is not only a fundamental strength of the social human, it is perhaps our single greatest survival advantage, over time. Human groups function best when the full range of cognitive styles is available, putting the full range of human decision-making and problem-solving at the disposal of the group. And on top of this, individual human beings function better, socially, when their turn of thought and reasoning are not implicitly obvious to others – when they must exercise their human connections by explaining why they see what they see and think what they think.

Did the Founders think of this? We have to conclude that they did; despite the uniformity of cognitive style among them as individuals, they were educated and perceptive enough to realize that people *do* think differently, person to person, and created deliberative processes and protocols that explicitly require lawmakers and other custodians of governance to engage one another and encounter each other's thoughts, rationales, and convictions – US government, put another way, enforces cognitive negotiation.

It's a cliché that the US is the greatest nation on earth – and of course, at this point in history there are many nations emulating our style of government, and many are doing a better job with it than we are. Who is and isn't great is for history to decide; but the *idea* of the United States, the concept of an EON Nation, is certainly among the greatest ideas ever conceived – and a game-changer for human society.

So Many Colors

When my younger two children (they are now 23 and 16) were in grade school at Montessori, I used to appear once a month or so with a guitar and spend an hour singing songs with their class. A favorite was a Harry Chapin song about creativity and the US education system, called "Flowers are Red" - but which came to be known as "The Montessori Song". Here's a key excerpt:

"Flowers are red, young man,
And green leaves are green;
There's no need to see flowers any other way
Than the way they always have been seen!"

But the little boy said,

There are so many colors in a rainbow,
So many colors in the morning sun,
So many colors in a flower,
And I see every one!"

The children would always join in loudly on that last part.

The point is this: per the cognitive framework discussed above, the teacher in the song is an ATU - telling the boy how to think (A), eschewing her own opportunity to learn (T) and shilling for the status quo (U).

The boy is an EON - pressing that his view is as valid as the authority figure's is (E), jumping on the opportunity to express a new frame (O), at the risk of earning social disapproval or even punishment - and seeing new possibilities (N).

Both of these characters come by their view naturally. Neither is "right," neither is "wrong," they simply see what they see. The tone of the song, of course, conveys disapproval that one of these characters attempts to impose their view upon the other, making the point that the educational system has been guilty of that. But we get the most from the lyric when we simply acknowledge the distinction in these views and understand what's in them.

This frame, simple as it is, covers just about everything we see around us today: the violence in Charlottesville, the confusion in the White House, the cacophonic collisions of frames and the roar of tempestuous worldviews. It's all as simple as the teacher and the boy.

I see what I see; you see what you see. That person over there, they see what they see. The liberal sees what she sees, the conservative sees what he sees; that conservationist sees what she sees, the atheist sees what he sees, those white nationalists see what they see.

We can't exactly switch eyes with other people. The very best we can hope for - and the thing we absolutely must pursue - is filling in the big picture for everyone. I see what I see, but there's a lot I'll never see, and that goes for you, too - and you, and you. All of us.

Our job is not to insist that what we see is all there is, and that what they see is wrong; our job is to realize that any one of us can only see in part, and only by filling in the picture together can we construct anything that can be called reality.

They always seem to win.

They believe themselves to believe the 'norm' - the '*true* Christians' - the '*real* Americans' - the 'Silent Majority'. They are the 'ideologically pure' that Rush Limbaugh seems to still believe in, the 'base'… the ones who vote, and vote relentlessly, for the Authoritarian.

They are, in the scientific notation of psychologist Robert Altemeyer, the High RWAs; adherents, in the nomenclature of cognitive linguist George Lakoff, of Strict Father Morality. They appear in every culture, the world over, now and back through history – and they always number, roughly, somewhere between 21 and 35 percent of any given population.

They always win.

Throughout history, the Authoritarian Follower has defined the course of human destiny. The leaders – social dominators, almost to the last! - who have harnessed endless populations of Authoritarian Followers throughout recorded history have been the dominant lever in humankind's moving of the earth. One can count the civilizations and nations and governments that were *not* Authoritarian by design on one hand (including, notably and thankfully, the United States).

Authoritarian Followers are a natural minority. The limbic emotions that enable their sociopolitical view of the world, and human nature, and their roles in their respective societies, are biologically predetermined – genetically linked, to do with the relative ratio of brain tissue in critical components of their limbic and cortical systems. And while this genetic predisposition is by no means the end-all-be-all of who we turn out to be – nurture and social circumstances are, of course, huge factors – we are usually raised around people who are like us, in sociopolitical worldview, so our innate impulses are, if anything, strengthened rather than changed.

If this is so, and if the genetics of it all set the rough number of Authoritarian personalities at about 1/3 - then why do Authoritarians and their socially dominant leaders rule others so often and so effortlessly?

It's pretty simple.

The 1/3 possess several key cognitive differences: 1) their level of discomfort with change, risk, and unfamiliar people is generally a good deal higher than the norm; 2) they see the world, in terms of resources/opportunity/survival, as a zero-sum domain; 3) their social frame overvalues social similarity, because group solidarity is seen as a survival key. Wrap this all into a single burrito, and it reads "Highly Competitive" on the menu.

The 2/3 is made up of everyone else – those who are not particularly uncomfortable with change, who are more willing to take risks, who are more comfortable with strangers. They see the world as perpetually renewing, rather than dangerous. Their social frame is more diverse, because they see more possible outcomes. They are more at ease with deciding together, rather than following a leader, and are more apt to work together across social boundaries. Wrap this all up in an enchilada, and it reads "Highly Cooperative" on the menu.

The thing is, both Competition and Cooperation are essential chapters in the human story. By and large we are at the very top of the tree of life, in terms of our capacity for cooperation – and, by and large, we ascended to that position by competing in the world against a vast array of creatures great and small who would have taken our place if they could.

But our competition *with each other* has held us back, and now threatens our continued ascendency.

How is this happening? If Cooperators are a reliable majority in every human population, how to Competitors continue to dominate? How can 2/3 lose, in the words of *The Newsroom*'s Will McAvoy, "so goddamn always?"

It takes but a moment's thought to get there.

What does the Competitor do, when offered cooperation? He pushes to win; he seeks to dominate, cooperation aside. He labors for 'one-party rule'; he rejects even those in his own tribe, if they do not share this goal; he divides the world into winners and losers, and Cooperators are, by definition, losers. Put another way, faced with the option to cooperate, he will compete – and relentlessly. Compromise is for the weak.

What does the Cooperator do, when offered competition? The Cooperator isn't interested in 'winning' and 'losing', s/he's interested in compromise – not a weakness, but a mutual accommodation; peaceful coexistence, negotiated progress. The Cooperator is a poor competitor; s/he makes for a pretty bland politician, and has a rough time rallying the party for decisive, confrontational action. The party isn't very interested in that.

Put another way, when faced with the option to complete, s/he will attempt to cooperate – and wind up, instead, 'losing'.

The Cooperator doesn't want to fight; the Competitor doesn't want to lose. This mix leads to the kind of environment we live in today – paralyzed, dysfunctional, indecisive, chaotic.

It would not be so, of course, if we – like so many societies before us – were straightforward Authoritarian. But we are something different: we are, by our Founding Fathers' arrangement, the ultimate experiment in Cooperative Authority – a society where Authority is arranged top-down (Authoritarian, at first glance), but with Authority deriving from the population itself (democracy – Egalitarian, at its core). This middle ground is our truest, best hope, perhaps the most ingenious approach to the 2/3 - 1/3 problem imaginable.

We need it to survive. We don't dare let it break down...

Dwelling

The Cro-Magnons had it easy.

100,000 years ago, there were no fantasy worlds. 100,000 years ago, there were no alternative human narratives into which human beings could retreat. 100,000 years ago, there was only one world - reality - within which to live one's life.

To begin with, there was no such thing as an "alternate narrative" prior to the development of spoken language. Human communication for the first 200,000 years of our species' existence was emotional (based on facial expression and vocal tone) and gestural (based on immediate reference to objects and events). Put simply, most of the human beings who have ever lived - although they each had an independent point of view - had no way to conceive of an alternative to the real-world human story, let alone communicate such a story to others.

But there's more to it: for a human narrative - a story explaining us to ourselves - to develop at all, there needs to be consensual human experience, including both shared and personal memories and references to the surrounding world, upon which to build. This process involves the human cognitive capacity to remember the past and imagine the future - abilities that we alone possess among living beings today, and which our hominin cousins could not match.

Given language and the sharing of experience, a human narrative can be constructed. And given the size of natural human communities (<150), such a narrative is achievable.

Cro-Magnons of the Upper Paleolithic, then, living in the final 30,000 years before the advent of civilization, may have been capable of creating such a narrative. But in a Cro-Magnon community, only one such narrative could exist, because such communities were so small that there was only one social group in the community - the community itself. It takes a few hundred people to generate distinct social groups within a single community (think junior high school, or your local church).

When a community is larger than a Cro-Magnon group could have been - from several hundred to several thousand - sub-groups can form within the community, which we've named cognitive clusters: sub-groups based on like-mindedness. And like-minded people can generate new narratives that deviate from the single, reality-based one that human communities once used.

Under the heel of a powerful leader, an entire nation can be forced to acquiesce to a state narrative (England throughout the Middle Ages), but even so, small-group counter-narratives will exist (the Protestants, the pagans). Different cognitive clusters will inevitably set up competing narratives, since the like-minded tend to see the world the same way and accept the same set of assumptions about human nature.

But even though such group narratives are completely satisfying and compelling to those within such a group, ALL of them are lacking; they over-emphasize those cherry-picked beliefs about self and others that make sense within the cognitive cluster, and de-emphasize those that don't. They edit reality to make it more emotionally appealing; they morph human nature into a distortion that exalts their group's strengths and excuses its weaknesses.

A reality-driven narrative is more honest, more fruitful, safer, and ultimately the choice of the emotionally mature - but it is, in the context of the social universe as it is today, the most difficult. To get there, one must depart from the narrative of one's sub-tribe, and go full Cro-Magnon - drawing reality from the totality of the surrounding others, bowing to the natural world, focusing on a human story that is more about what we actually see and hear and less about what we imagine or desire or wish.

It's difficult to admit that we were better at this when we were cave dwellers - but when we were cave dwellers, we didn't plunder each other, enslave each other or slaughter each other in the name of some god. Cave dwellers did one thing really well: they dwelled, and dwelling is a community thing.

Doesn't that sound good?

The Fact-Based World

It's both intriguing and informative, as a scientist, to spend some time each day in the subjective milieu of the Internet, watching people of all sorts sift thru reality like Walmart shoppers on a mission.

And it's disheartening to realize that we have, as a species, become so detached from what's real and what's not that it is possible to spend a lifetime within fantasy constructs, viewing neither ourselves nor those around us as what we really are.

I have accepted a new professional role, and it's also a social role: I have joined a company that studies medical, demographic and lifestyle information about pregnant women in order to better insure that they carry their babies safely to term.

The science of this mission is called analytics: the deep analysis of large bodies of data in pursuit of patterns that reveal information otherwise undetected. In this case, it is to discover events and conditions that cause premature birth, in order to avoid them. The consequences of successful outcomes in this mission are profound: the mother/family avoid trauma; the child is more likely to be strong and healthy, and avoid a potential lifetime of difficulty and misery; and the savings in medical expense are far more than you might guess.

The *only* path to success in this mission, for me and my colleagues, is strict adherence to what's real. Most laypeople take license to redefine science in such a way as to make it something it isn't, which is vexing to those of us who live within it - but the rules of science are not only clear but firm: indulgence of wishful thinking, bias or personal agenda is a fast track to failure.

There are no ideological concerns here. Illusions about the biological realities of human beings are pointless. And, most importantly, armchair psychology about what goes on in the mind of a pregnant woman is far out of bounds. All of these cognitive junk foods, which almost everyone chomps on daily on Facebook, have no place within my company's work - or, by extension, science in general.

This takes us into the question of how it could be productive, or even desirable, to construct fantasy worlds atop the real one - why we so eagerly play make-believe, when it comes to who and what we are, and the nature of those with whom we share the world. It is not overstating to say that this tendency is at the heart of most of our disheartening, creepy social dysfunction, and the tragedies we've observed over the past week: they are a result of indulgence in fantasies about who we are and aren't.

But that's for another day. Today's point is simple: focusing on the real world generates real results - in my own case, I'm hoping, life-changing results. I'll take that, with all the hard work it entails, over junk-food fantasies any day.

"If there is danger in the human trajectory, it is not so much in the survival of our own species as in the fulfillment of the ultimate irony of organic evolution - that in the instant of achieving self-understanding through the mind of man, life has doomed its most beautiful creations."

-Edward O. Wilson

A Woman and a Man

There's the hilarious riff that men's brains are full of mutually-exclusive boxes, while women's brains are big balls of wire: males tend to compartmentalize their lives, in other words, while women tend to connect all the facets of their lives.

What's going on here is neurological. Female primates have 20 percent more connective tissue in the corpus callosum - that segment of the brain that joins the two hemispheres together - and thus enjoy far greater communication of signals across hemispheres. Put another way, they tend to connect their perceptions and memories in their conscious thought because that's what's literally happening, among their neurons. And men - not so much. Or not *as* much, to be more accurate.

Why is he telling us this?

I'm telling you this because it's yet another example of how one human being's inner experience can be so different from another's, when our outer lives seem to be filled with all the same things - in particular, when a man and a woman are sharing their lives.

When a woman and a man truly love one another and have created, between them, the partnership we think of as couplehood, their outer lives truly do merge: they begin and end each day together, they spend as much of it in one another's company as is practical, they eat together, they communicate and share what's happening when they're apart - they are experiencing the same day, to a large degree, with only minor differences. Yet even so, they can move through the same day together and process the day completely differently - one has a good day and the other a bad day, even though it's much the same day.

And this is where true couplehood emerges: the man learns that even though his own mind can't do what hers can - connecting each event to a memory, each memory to a feeling, and each feeling to another - he can observe and appreciate that she is doing exactly that, and enjoy it, even though it's not what's happening within himself. Likewise, the woman learns that the man's ability to organize his inner world like his garage workbench is natural - and, moreover, a help to her and to the relationship, as it empowers him to embrace multiple roles in her life: not just lover, but best friend; not just companion, but guardian.

She achieves the same for him in exactly the opposite way, through her inner connectivity; but the bottom line is that if it were otherwise, they could not be what they are to one another. The difference between the brain of the woman and the brain of the man is an adaptation that makes our not-particularly-natural monogamy a practical objective.

And it's that way with all human relationships: we don't need to share the experience of another precisely in order to share in the pleasure that their experience brings them. We call that 'empathy', and we could all use a lot more of it...

Connection, Not Correction

Feelings, not facts. I participated in a discussion yesterday where the Extreme Right's imperviousness to facts was being lamented, as it so often is, with much bemoaning and teeth-gnashing and bottomless frustration. And having spent the previous week arguing passionately for a cessation of this deepening conflict over fact/fake, a noose that only tightens in the struggle, I offered an alternative.

Correction hasn't worked here, and never can. The wholesale rejection of fact, the tendency of the extreme group to set aside reality for a contrived alternative, is an unassailable feature of that group's dynamic; it isn't passive, it isn't incidental, it's built into the fabric of their universe. No amount of evidence, no amount of intellectual pressure or disapproval from without will ever tip them back toward objective truth: they don't want or need it, and the constant parade from those who would school them only pushes them farther away.

Correction isn't the answer, and can't be achieved, even if it were. The problem is not that groups in denial are in denial; the problem of groups in denial is that they are groups.

These are people who are bonded to one another because they have found their worldview and their ideas and feelings to be demeaned by those who do not share them. There is truth in that - those not on the Extreme Right *do*find its worldview ugly and harsh, and their ideas and feelings are decidedly unattractive - and it is natural for such a group to actively distance themselves from those who stand apart.

Their bonds grow stronger and stronger, the more opposition is mounted against them. Facts will never make a difference; "fake" will be their mantra. And the more righteous they feel, the more they will isolate - and, feeling themselves to be threatened (even in abstract) will only make them more militant.

This is a high-gain loop; no group starts out this way. This is the echo chamber on steroids, The Who playing the Grand Canyon: opposition becomes fuel. It has less and less to do with facts, or even ideology, and more and more to do with social distance - broken community, with our human bonds far more severed than our intellectual bonds.

Connection is the answer to this problem, not correction. Restoring the civility of human contact, the bridge of shared humanity - the truth that the reassurance of benign interaction with another can change the tone of our day and soothe the distress of inner problems - that's what can reach the unreachable.

When we step on an elevator or hold the door for someone at the mall, we don't know their political tribe, and we don't care - they are just another human being, and that's enough. I propose that this is a higher truth than our deep political convictions and high-sounding rhetoric. Connection on a human level can and should transcend our internal social biases.

That connection is easy to achieve, even in the context of an impersonal Internet and a flame-friendly arena of political discourse. It is the work of a moment to set aside "I am right because of these facts," and say instead, "The problem we're discussing makes me feel..." Expressing how one feels to another opens a door, taking both to the bridge of shared experience. It doesn't matter that our feelings aren't the same; what's important is that our feelings about the issues that divide us are the thing that truly binds us: we feel, all of us, and we all know the power and intensity of that experience. Sharing it makes one less an opponent and more a neighbor.

This technique doesn't solve problems; by definition, it can't, because it doesn't address the issues. Instead, it changes the conversation, making it more about who we are and how we feel, and less about what we want and why we're right. It doesn't strengthen our position or our arguments - but it does strengthen us and those we engage with it. It puts the focus in the place where it ultimately belongs - our shared stake in the future, and our need to be more firmly connected to one another than to our biases.

And it skips us over so much pointless strife and stress and useless rancor. Isn't that alone reason enough to give it a try?

People are Complicated

People are complicated.

Partisanism is not.

Science is difficult.

Denial is not.

Relationships are demanding.

Abandonment is not.

Vulnerability is costly.

Detachment is not.

Compassion is loving.

Snark is not.

"Centuries of centuries, and only in the present do things happen."

-Jorge Luis Borges

Venturing Out

Often we resist–or are attracted to–a social truth, not based on its merits or weaknesses, but because of how it makes us feel… and, often, we are not consciously aware of it. This is particularly problematic in science, where practitioners are as subject to this impulse as any of us.

(Aside: non-scientists frequently feel the freedom to criticize science on this basis, saying scientists are just as human and mistake-prone as any of us. No. They are not nearly as mistake-prone, or they wouldn't have been able to achieve their post; and, though they do have internal biases, they don't even get the word out on their work unless they get past an army of pit bulls who *don't* share their biases. That's what makes it science.)

This quest for social comfort/safety can cause us to make compromises in our personal lives that we might not want, and might step around if not for that discomfort. Religions play on those discomforts, amplifying the dangers waiting beyond the group beyond reason, while exaggerating the level of social acceptance and commitment offered to the individual. This, too, would be ineffective, if the social universe at large didn't feel so unsafe.

The bottom line is that no one wants to be alone. An individual may enjoy solitude, but that doesn't mean they invite rejection; a rare few self-isolate to the point of neurosis, but they didn't come by that impulse without some serious pain.

The objective truth of the social human is that we obtain our "I" from others; our brains are wired for connection with other human beings, our self-knowledge and our understanding of the world and our own lives derives from those connections. The objective truth of our existence is that other people aren't "hell"; they're our greatest asset - and, ideally, our greatest joy.

The groups we join intensify that reality, making it easier to feel; and we scramble to feel it, in a world full of strangers, for which our brains are unprepared. For the better part of a year now, we've been talking about the science of this, not just the subjective feel-good aspects; group membership is simultaneously our personal salvation and our crippling foe.

More often than not, the choice of groups we join is made for us - church, school, workplace - we have little control over who we grow up among, or who we must deal with every day. And when we do have choices, we are generally motivated by impulses we aren't even aware of.

Too seldom do we simply sit in the park and greet strangers and enjoy passive participation in the lives of others. Too seldom do we reflect on the fullness of humanity that we miss, sheltered within the confines of fake tribes.

The danger isn't in venturing out; the danger is in *not*venturing out...

"There is a cult of ignorance in the United States, and there always has been, nurtured by the false notion that democracy means that 'my ignorance is just as good as your knowledge.'"

~Isaac Asimov

Is Humanism a Religion?

The religious love to say so; the idea that 'atheists' (whatever that means) are surrendering despite themselves to a supposedly universal human impulse to embrace the divine is irresistible to them.

But humanists will invariably respond and clarify that the entire point of their belief system is that they wish to direct their spiritual energies (whatever that means) into the betterment of humankind, not the adulation of some wispy, contrived ghost figure; they are humanists precisely because they want human beings to rely upon human beings, and not upon wishful thinking.

Still, the humanist overlaps considerably with the theist in a number of key areas.

The humanist acts from conviction. Like the theist, the humanist cultivates a deep belief in the mission of the belief, and allows that belief to serve as guide. Most humanists are as committed to humanism as their theist counterparts are committed to their religions, if not more. And this deep conviction spurs them to action.

The humanist revels in the company of peers. Just as the theist is more socially comfortable among other theists, the humanist is most at ease among other humanists. This, of course, is cognitive clustering, and it works against the humanist even more than it does the theist, to the point of irony. All the same, it is a noteworthy commonality.

The humanist deeply believes in the ultimate utility of the belief. The religious look to the heavens for salvation from imagined calamities, and that gaze seldom wavers; deep is the certainty that Only My Religion Can Save Us All. The humanist looks around, not up, but feels the same; only humanism can secure the human future.

But the humanist breaks with the theist on a key point. The theist derives deep joy from belief in a deity, and the sharing of that belief with others. The theist will regularly join together in tribal community, celebrating the belief, entering into collective euphoria, celebrating that binding conviction. The humanist has no such celebration, and thus no such joy.

This is a critical missing piece. The humanist is a step ahead, intellectually and even spiritually (whatever that means), and has every reason to celebrate - but doesn't. The humanist has all the motivation in the world to gather with others in ritual joy - but doesn't.

The counter-argument is that the joy of religious ecstasy is a false euphoria, and that the theist is invested in the celebration of fantasy. But isn't most euphoria false? Isn't most euphoria contrived, puffed up out of abstraction, generated for its own sake? Holidays, calendar landmarks, rites of passage - don't we manufacture them all, simply because we enjoy the communal act of celebration? Does it matter that these things are pure invention?

The humanist needs celebration, joy, euphoria - for the humanist, of all of those who are reverent before an ideal, have cause: nothing is more wondrous, more awe-inspiring, more worthy of fealty and celebration than humankind. Cultivating that missing piece might seem to bolster the notion of humanism as a religion, but so be it: it might also make devotion to our kind, and the creation of a safe and robust future, moving forward, a more common priority.

"The image of humanity, warped by bloodlust, inevitably marching off to kill, is a powerful myth and an important prop of militarism in our society. Despite its lack of scientific credibility, there will remain those 'hard-headed realists' who continue to believe in it, congratulating themselves for their 'courage to face the truth,' resolutely oblivious to the myth behind their 'reality.'"

~R. Brian Ferguson

Angry Birds

I count among my friends three intellectual curmudgeons, all senior to me in both years and curmudgeoning, all members in good standing of a curmudgeons' coffee club that has been going strong for a quarter century. They are fun fellows, each razor-sharp of mind and wit, deeply committed to reason and critical thought, and each in turns either amused or disturbed at the perpetual follies of lesser minds.

Amused and disturbed, they extend their discussion from the coffee shop to email, where I find almost daily exchanges gleefully excoriating this or that Fundamentalist buffoon. Lots of this glee is a burning-off of excess outrage over Tea Party antics and the Evangelical revisions of the beloved Framers; but it has extended, for over two decades, to public debate of Creationists, and this is where my eyebrow goes up.

It's one thing to kid around among friends, or to forward funny emails. It's another thing altogether to go out among the masses, performing the funny emails as community theater.

It's not that I don't think their cause is righteous. Anything that preserves the sanctity of the public school classroom is better than the reverse, and I'm every bit as amused and disturbed by the tent revival chants and howls as they; but *debate*? Really?

It's not just that debating Creationists is about as sporting as hunting cows; it's that debate itself is one of our greatest social and intellectual treasures, all the way back to ancient Greece, Persia and beyond. What happens in a Creationist debate is an assault upon its dignity, an assault that raises the credibility of the Creationist by his very admission into its shadow. (This is why Richard Dawkins won't indulge in it.)

And if the subject matter is unfit for the forum, the practitioners are even moreso. Any system of thought that places William Lane Craig and Kirk Cameron on equal footing can't truly be called a system of thought. Debate tests the strengths of arguments; it also tests the strength of arguers. My friends can't even work up a sweat, and they know it going in.

I'm not going to spend time on the why of it, apart from a single statement that the substance of these 'debates' doesn't conform to the rules, let alone the intent, of the process of debate. The two sides are talking about two completely different things, and pretending this isn't so doesn't make it so. The process of debate was not designed to reconcile this kind of difference in propositions.

To me, the Evolution-Creation problem is about something else entirely, and can't be addressed, let alone solved, on the debate floor – and this is why I have concerns over my friends making a public pastime of it. Their doing so calls to mind my youngest daughter playing Angry Birds, that iPhone game with the slingshot and the pellet-like birds, raining down destruction on the pigs. As the most successful app ever, at a billion downloads and counting, Angry Birds has managed to justify video games under the distinction that every video game since Pong has suffered, but which we never spoke aloud: *time-waster*.

Debating Creationists is an intellectual time-waster, on a par with speed chess, *Star Trek*, and Michael Crichton novels.

Even so, what of it? Would I scold my pals for reading *Sphere*? Or, for that matter, playing Angry Birds?

It's about the time, yes, but it's more about the knowledge and brainpower. My buddies have some serious intellectual game, and more important, serious commitment. The more of those things we can muster today, the better off we'll all be in the long run. From their point of view, of course, the time isn't wasted; they are making an earnest effort to change minds that have been misled; they are adding dignity to an otherwise ludicrous public discourse, rather than diminishing the integrity of debate; and most importantly, they're fighting for what they believe in.

They remind me of the numbers: according to Gallop, as of Dec. 2010, almost 40 percent of the US population believes in Creationism (that number includes slightly more than half of all Republicans). My response: What was the number 50 years ago? 100? 500? Hasn't it changed radically, even staggeringly, and isn't it going in the right direction?

See? We're making a difference, they say, and I shake my head. You're changing minds? People come up to you after these debates and say, *You really sold me?* Well … no, they admit, although every so often they get a follow-up email from someone who has been pushed out of the nest at some point, and that person expresses appreciation for what they're doing. Even so, they insist, the Religious Right is pushing so hard with its Creationist campaign, many who are undecided on the Evolution/Creation quest will be swayed the wrong way.

The numbers say we can breathe easy on this one: among those who attend church seldom or never, says Gallop, the number of people who buy Creationism is only a third of those who don't. And we have little reason to worry that these people are going to join up anytime soon: whatever Evangelicals tell themselves, and despite Billy Graham's best efforts, the statistical truth is that only one church member out of every five was not raised in the church.

The rate of Evangelical apostasy, on the other hand, is now over one in four – a net loss for Evangelical rolls – and a number that more than accounts for the thank-you emails my friends receive.

But these aren't the numbers that compel me, here. The recent findings of neuroscience, based on fMRI studies of the neurological nature of Belief, show us a picture that tells us what we're up against, when people believe really bizarre things: there is no significant difference, neurologically, between a life-long belief and a life-long habit. In the bedrock of neurons and synapses, it is all about long-term potentiation, and we now have many studies that include real-time brain scans that show us how 'belief' works, as a brain function, and in particular, what other cognitive processes it resembles.

If I have a life-long 'belief' that has been potentiating in my neurons for decades, and someone confronts me with new information that overturns the belief, the new information does no more to alter my potentiated synapses than does the cancer warning label on the cigarette pack of the life-long smoker.

Ah, William Lane Craig or Kirk Cameron might object, but if 'belief' is so permanent, why do scientists so readily abandon theirs?

Two reasons. First, scientists do not 'abandon' their belief in the knowledge Science has provided them: they *modify* it, and that modification tends to be slight, and incremental. Second, scientists do not have their knowledge constantly re-potentiated into concrete by their peers. The community of Science is a place wherein it is understood by all (the behaviors of the cantankerous aside) that *all Knowledge is transitory*. Those who participate understand that they must hold all their treasures loosely. Neurologically, this translates into a much more moderate potentiation of the states of the brain that embody Knowledge.

It's also true that there's quite a spectrum of variability in this neurological picture. Among people who derive their identity, their sense of who they are, from the social group they belong to (in this case, the Evangelical church) – the neurological power of Belief is going to be far, far stronger. So those who do renounce Creationism are, statistically, neuro-lite to begin with.

But … we live in Kentucky, my friends howl, where those nuts have built that Temple of the Flintstones, the 'Creationist Museum,' and the state's governor is actually promoting it!

Well, okay, that's irritating, to be sure; but the Flintstone Temple isn't going to change any minds in either direction, and Gov. Beshear has acted on behalf of tourism, not theology or anti-Science. Kenneth Ham built it, let them come, with their out-of-state revenue. Kentucky can surely use the money (I'm sure Congressman Yarmuth has some suggestions on how to spend it …).

So – if my really smart, really committed friends want to make a difference, what should they be doing instead?

Consider that the slam-down of Creationism on educational policy is a symptom, not a cause. For almost thirty years, this slam-down has been in progress, affecting not just education but almost every facet of public policy. Those who actively spoon-feed Evangelicals spread distrust of Science and intellect far beyond ninth-grade biology class. This spreading has been systematic and persistent, and has resulted in a national gestalt, regarding empirical truth, that is unique among the industrialized nations.

Why? Because people who question, who challenge authority, who demand evidence, are much harder to control. Those who would have power over the voter have to work much harder when the voter requires that the decisions of policy-makers be supported by objective evidence. Science bows to no single authority, but requires the same scrupulous, honest standards of all. That's a tough room to work, for unscrupulous leaders.

If given the choice between playing Angry Birds and leaving William Lane Craig and Kirk Cameron to their fate, I'd turn another direction, and pour all of my energy, knowledge and perspective into those who already grant the veracity of Science and the lunacy of Creationism, but who spend their weekends playing speed chess, watching old *Star Trek* and reading Michael Crichton.

I'd focus on mobilizing those minds that can be mobilized, not bothering with those minds that can't be changed, realizing that more mobilized minds inevitably protect public policy from the unchangeable ones.
No more Angry Birds! Start feeding real ones.

The power of reason, empiricism, and shared knowledge has proven itself over and over again over the past three centuries, to the good of all, and to the detriment of the powerful. But in every case, that proof has emerged on the far side of endless struggle against the emotionally-charged forces of dogmatism, the inevitable insecurities of change and the ferocious machinations of those who hold sway over the good natures of the deeply community-minded.

How wonderful, how reassuring and miraculous it would be if those forces and insecurities and machinations would yield, per nature's laws, to the disciplines of reason, shared observation, the benign meeting of minds for mutual benefit. How gentle and strong and safe we all could become, if the young and vigorous leaps and landings of empiricism were as pervasive and resilient as the ancient neural thunder of fear and tribe.

But … that turns out not to be the case.

Adulting

John Shelby Spong, the ultra-progressive Episcopalian priest, is famous for his proclamation that "Hell" is an invention of Christian church leaders, to keep the Christian masses in fear. And the point of the fear, he has said, is control: keep people afraid, and you can control them.

"Religion is always in the control business," he said, "and that something that most people don't really understand. It's in the guilt-producing control business. [Hell] is part of a control tactic.

"The church doesn't like for people to grow up," he continued, "because you can't control grown-ups."

Let's save Hell and the church for another time. Let's look at this idea that people who control entire populations of other people do so by cultivating their fear and suppressing their adulting.

Let's start with the realization that, well, it works. A vast group of calm, quiet, perfectly normal and happy people can be whipped into a fearful frenzy that sweeps them into the streets with pitchforks and torches, yanking their Other-ethnic neighbors into the trees at the end of nooses. As Steven Weinberg put it, "With or without religion, you would have good people doing good things and evil people doing evil things; but for good people to do evil things - that takes religion."

Make People Afraid: it's been a cornerstone of politics for thousands of years. Tyrants, despots, preachers and other control mongers have long kept it within arm's reach, the most effective bludgeon in their arsenal for assaulting reason. Make people afraid, and many will cast about for someone to save them, to protect them, to make them feel secure. It is the social dominator's bridle and saddle.

But Fear is not the only tool for keeping people in line.

Adults often continue to act like children when they are perpetually treated like children, for instance.

This tactic kept America's slave population in check for centuries. We are reminded of the exchange between wealthy Northerner George Hazard and wealthy Southerner Orry Main in John Jakes' "North and South" - two friends divided over the slavery issue (Orry's family has many of them) in the years preceding the Civil War:

"Just look at them, George," Orry argues, "they can't read or write, they can't think straight, they'd be lost without us! They're like children!"

"Yes," George agrees, "-because we keep them so."

It's the same today - not with African-Americans and not with the church, but with those with whom we disagree politically.

Our over-amped rhetoric, our constant state of bidirectional provocation, our seemingly infinite reservoir of derision and contempt - all are tuned to framing our opponents as immature, incapable of independent thought, beyond the reach of adult reason and autonomous decision. My question: doesn't this set up a self-justifying prophesy?

If the goal is to draw those who cluster around the podium of the despot out into the fresh air of adult autonomy and independent thought, does it help to treat them like children?

If the goal is to break the spell of the social dominator, to lure the spell-bound away from the faux security and lullaby of groupthink into the robust comforts and challenges of adult awareness, isn't it utterly counterproductive to taunt them with schoolyard rants and demeaning name-calling?

Human beings generally start adulting when they have the need, the encouragement and the freedom to do so. Provisioning for oneself creates the need; family and friends provide the encouragement; and freedom to step out into the world includes feeling confident and safe in doing so.

When a despot or president or preacher is obscuring that need to think for oneself, we only make matters far worse when we push such people away, rather than invite them in, when we present an outer terrain populated with scorn and ridicule, rather than interest and receptivity.

My very loud friends need to take a deep breath. While they have not only the freedom but the obligation to continue to protest both policies and behaviors that harm others, they need to not just dial down but let go altogether the terrible rhetoric they are hurling toward people themselves: they need to realize that their self-righteous bellowing is only entrenching their opposition, lining up votes for the other side, amplifying the hatred.

They need to take a second deep breath, get ahold of themselves, resolve to start listening as earnestly as they protest, and reach out an authentically welcoming hand.

That's what adults do.

The Good Book

When you think about it - it really is a Good Book.

It is a book endlessly talked about, but seldom read in full.

It takes us from the dawn of time to our current contemplations. It draws us in with the story of where we come from, and ends with who we will become.

It offers us the human narrative in all its splendor, with all its warts. It is an encyclopedia of human discovery and human struggle, soundtracked with both the drums of war and the pipes of peace, illuminated by the light of wonder. It satiates our hunger to know.

It tells of our journey into darkness, step by step through the eons - of our ugliness to one another, our thirst for power, our indifference to our brother's suffering. It unveils our most shameful moments - slavery, violence, betrayal - the full flower of human greed and dishonesty.

It is a Good Book, but a frankone - it spares us not at all, disclosing our inhumanity and selfishness as it struggles to hold up our ultimate hopes and most noble dreams. And it culminates with the fate of our savior, the offering up of an innocent - the best of us! - to face the fiery pit, to do ultimate battle with the ultimate evil, emerging to assure us that we have been saved, then to vanish into light.

It is the story of humankind, of our deep spiritual disease and our ultimate salvation. It is our cornerstone, the bedrock of our understanding of ourselves.

From our modern perspective, we simply can't take it literally. We know that while it holds the general shape of human history, it just isn't accurate: the peoples and events it chronicles, the times and places, just don't match up with what we know to be true. It can't all be fact; even within the text itself, the contradictions are many.

It presents a diverse humanity, an accidental landscape populated not only with people as we are today, but with subtle storybook variations that earlier readers were too naive to dismiss. It features creatures we now realize are purely mythical. It parades magicks that are not real, presuming mysticism as humanity's default perspective - untenable in our age of reason.

Its many stories and characters compel us, nonetheless. We can't take it literally, but we can take it seriously. It can guide us, and guide us well, as we wander into tomorrow.

Myth? Perhaps. But even so, it is a book that shows us who we really are - from the very worst of our tainted nature to the very best we are capable of being.

It is a book no home should be without, a book everyone should read, discuss, and embrace.

Thank you, JRR Tolkien...

About the Author

Scott Robinson is a journalist, social scientist, public speaker and musician, and was for 20 years a music critic with the *Louisville Courier-Journal*. He has also been published in *Rolling Stone* and *The Wall Street Journal*. He can be found at**www.facebook.com/scottrobinson99**.